Joe Orton

Twayne's English Authors Series

Kinley Roby, Editor

Northeastern University

TEAS 515

JOE ORTON IN 1966.
Photo courtesy of John Haynes.

Joe Orton

Susan Rusinko

Bloomsburg University of Pennsylvania, Emeritus

Twayne Publishers • New York
An Imprint of Simon & Schuster Macmillan

Prentice Hall International
London Mexico City New Delhi Singapore Sydney Toronto

Twayne's English Authors Series No. 515

Joe Orton
Susan Rusinko

Twayne Publishers
An Imprint of Simon & Schuster Macmillan
866 Third Avenue
New York, New York 10022

Library of Congress Cataloging-in-Publication Data

Rusinko, Susan.
    Joe Orton / Susan Rusinko.
        p.   cm—(Twayne's English authors series ; TEAS 515)
    Includes bibliographical references and index.
    ISBN 0-8057-7034-8 (alk. paper)
    1. Orton, Joe—Criticism and interpretation.   I. Title.   II. Series.
PR6065.R7Z84   1995
822'.914—dc20   95-10064
                                                                                        CIP

10 9 8 7 6 5 4 3 2 1

Printed in the United States of America

Contents

Preface

Joe Orton, whose violent death at the age of 34 shocked the theatrical world in 1967, seemed relegated by critics to the status of a promising playwright cut short in his ascendancy. That his ascendancy was cut short is a fact. That at his death he was only "promising" has been contradicted by the steadily growing posthumous success of his plays.

Of a 1993 production of *Entertaining Mr. Sloane,* Julian Duplain wrote in the *Times Literary Supplement* that Orton's 1964 play still had an edge,

even if the comic shock of carnal scheming in suburbia has been dulled by almost three decades of television satire and social liberalization. Some lines, however, are so well written that, like Wildean aphorisms, they have taken on a life outside of their original context and it is a surprise to discover their source. When Kath longs for Sloane to be present at the birth of their baby, her brother Ed . . . observes, "It's enough for most children if the father is there at the conception." And a line like "You showed him the gates of hell every night—he abandoned all hope when he entered there," still gathers laughs for its urbane daring in mixing art and smut.[1]

At his death Orton had written only three long stage plays, four short plays for radio and television (two later revised for the stage), one novel published posthumously, one published but unproduced film script for the Beatles, one brief sketch for Kenneth Tynan's *Oh, Calcutta!,* and his posthumously published *Diaries.* He lived to enjoy three years of stage successes with *Entertaining Mr. Sloane* and *Loot,* despite the moral wrath called down on him by some critics, the public, and indeed, Mrs. Edna Welthorpe, Orton's own epistolary persona whose hypocrisy echoed that of some of his critics.

In a review of *Entertaining Mr. Sloane,* the first of Orton's stage plays, Alan Brien of the *Sunday Telegraph* spoke of him as "one of those rare dramatists who create their own world in their own idiom. A new generation is treading on the heels of those grand old men of the fifties, Harold Pinter and John Osborne."[2] Brien's characterization has been confirmed and expanded in the years following Orton's death.

Twenty years after Orton's death, Maurice Charney, in a creative analysis of Orton's linguistic uniqueness, placed him in the company of his contemporaries Harold Pinter and Tom Stoppard. All three—Pinter, Orton, and Stoppard—have acquired adjectival status as having created a new language for the stage. All three belong to the tradition of James Joyce and Samuel Beckett, as reinvigorators of stage language not in evidence since the Renaissance.

All five writers have their roots in one kind of exile or another. Joyce and Beckett chose to leave Ireland for the Continent, returning rarely to their native soil yet earning their place in the literary history on the basis of the idiom of the very culture they had abandoned. Exile and cunning, the tools of Stephen Dedalus in Joyce's *Portrait of the Artist as a Young Man,* are the means by which he resolves to encounter the reality of experience for the millionth time and to forge within the smithy of his soul the uncreated conscience of his race.

Exiles—albeit ones who have remained in their own country—is a key word to understanding the importance of Pinter, Stoppard, and Orton, for all three in one sense or another share a foreignness. Pinter's Jewish origins and his having been born and educated in the Hackney section of North London are imprinted on all he has written, particularly in the reticence and silences with which his characters deal with Kafkaesque menaces. Stoppard's exile is primarily geographical. Having come to England from Czechoslovakia via Singapore and Darjeeling after World War II (with his early education at an American school in Darjeeling), he embraced his adopted country. Kenneth Tynan once characterized him as more English than the English and as someone who thought there was no greater honor than to be born English. His luxuriating in the potential of his adopted language is everywhere evident in his plays.

Orton's origins, on the other hand, are very English. Of lower-middle-class society in a very middle-class English city, Leicester, he chose exile from Leicester to London (and Tangier) rather than having it imposed on him by accident of birth or circumstance. A sexual, social, and artistic exile, he transformed the clichés of middle-class vernacular into an art form. He belongs to the rebellious tradition of such writers as Ben Jonson, Christopher Marlowe (who died a violent death at an even earlier age than did Orton), William Wycherley, and William Congreve (whom Orton especially admired for threatening to give up the stage after the failure of *The Way of the World*). Like that of Joyce and Beckett, Orton's rebellion took shape only when, at the age of 17, he left Leicester for good.

As abused as the adjectives *Pinteresque, Stoppardian,* and *Ortonesque* may be, they do conjure up for audiences and readers the distinctions that define the fictional universe of each writer. Their respective idioms consist of Pinter's minimalist verbiage, with its famous pauses and silences, intended to hold at bay real and imagined threats to a character's existence; Stoppard's skyrocketing linguistic images, designed to release fantasies and frustrations; and Orton's epigrammatic speech patterns, aimed, with deadly accuracy, at the hilariously built-in contradictions between private needs and public expression of those needs in perversely deployed logic and language.

Pinter, as he himself has said, uses language and silence to reveal the poverty within the characters—that poverty involving unending psychological contests in which power is constantly shifting from one character to another. Stoppard's language consists of exotic metaphors, sharp wit, and abundant literary allusions to depict man's building and dismantling of logical structures—in philosophy, ethics, politics, love, and science. Orton's stage idiom shapes the banal into aphoristic high art, in a collage (his own term) of clichés and devilishly turned logic to communicate an ultimate outrage that can find expression only in the techniques of the clown. His characters release one irrational impulse after another and justify their behavior in axiomatic language that expresses Orton's perverse disregard for hypocritical authority, be it sexual mores, corporate mentality, religion, psychiatry, the police, the Islington library, or such national heroes as Winston Churchill.

Anarchy and subversiveness are Orton's aesthetic versions of the "cunning and exile" adopted by Joyce's Stephen Dedalus. Their literal manifestations are sexual, both in Orton's insistently subversive personal life and in the publicly flaunted aggressions of his characters. Sexual perversity is Orton's chosen metaphor for his gleeful thrashing of authority. In this respect he extends existing boundaries even as he stays within the confines of conventional farce, in which happy endings for the characters prevail, however socially demeaning and perverse their nature.

Orton's idiom is brilliantly argued from the perspective of the clown—the ultimate form of chosen exile—by John Lahr in his authorized biography of Orton. Maurice Charney explores the language of Orton in the context of traditional farce—the occultic discourse in *Entertaining Mr. Sloane,* the quotidian farce in *Loot,* and the seventeenth-century style of black comedy that unites the sexually energetic Old Comedy of Aristophanes with the New Comedy of Plautus, with its "careful intrigue plotting." These Charney sees as joining forces with the "self-conscious, parodic, histrionic clowning of modern black comedy in the style of Beckett, Pinter, Ionesco, Stoppard, and Brecht."[3]

In posthumous productions and critical evaluations, Orton's reputation has gained momentum, so that, however, brief his life and work, he has earned a place among the major reinventors of language on the English stage.

The chapters are arranged chronologically, in order of performance or publication of Orton's plays. Given the haphazard reception of his work, however—for instance, *Loot* failed in its initial pre-London production and was successfully produced the next year, *What the Butler Saw* failed and then succeeded in broadly similar fashion, and his productions failed in New York only to enjoy success in the second round—any attempt to assemble a chronology of Orton's plays risks confusion. There are some confusing lapses of time among the writing, rewriting, and productions—failed and successful—of the plays. My intent here is to follow the progression of Orton's three major plays as they move from the naturalistic comedy of manners (*Entertaining Mr. Sloane*) to a farcical comedy of manners (*Loot*) and, finally, to pure farce (*What the Butler Saw*). Other of Orton's published writings—*The Orton Diaries*, his four short plays (*The Ruffian on the Stair, The Good and Faithful Servant, The Erpingham Camp*, and *Funeral Games*), his novel (*Head to Toe*), a sketch for Tynan's *Oh, Calcutta!* (*Until She Screams*), and his film script for the Beatles (*Up Against It*)—are discussed as important works of an oeuvre that is at its Ortonesque best in his last long play.

Acknowledgments

Once more I acknowledge the generous help of two colleagues, Virginia Duck and Gerald Strauss, who over the years have served doubly as proofreaders and listeners. Their substantive and stylistic suggestions are much appreciated. I value the incisive copyediting by Barbara Sutton and the congenial help of the staff at the Harvey A. Andruss Library at Bloomsburg University—Josephine Crossley, Alice Getty, Monica Howell, Alex Shiner, and the acquisitions librarian Aaron Polonsky.

Permission to quote from *The Complete Plays of Joe Orton* and *The Diaries of Joe Orton* has been granted by Reed Consumer Books and by Grove/Atlantic.

I thank Jerry Goodstein and Anita and Steve Shevett for their photographs of American productions of Orton's plays and the Billy Rose Theater Collection at the New York Public Library for help in providing names and photographs. For scenes from London productions, I am grateful to photographers John Haynes and David Montgomery and to the Angus McBean Estate, the Theatre Museum at Covent Garden, and to Geoffrey Davies for his help as a London liaison.

Chronology

1959   Moves into flat purchased by Halliwell at 25 Noel Road, Islington; with Halliwell begins defacing library books.

1960   Collaborates with Halliwell on the novel version of *The Boy Hairdresser* (unpublished).

1961   Writes the novel *The Vision of Gombold Proval*, published posthumously as *Head to Toe;* submits *The Visit* to the Royal Court Theatre in London.

1962   On 5 May is arrested, with Halliwell, for damaging library books; they spend six months in jail, first at Wormwood Scrubs and then Orton at H. M. Prison East Church, Sheerness, Kent, and Halliwell at H. M. Prison, Arundel, Sussex.

1963   In August sells *The Ruffian on the Stair* (originally *The Boy Hairdresser*) to the BBC; in September–December writes *Entertaining Mr. Sloane;* in December acquires a literary agent, Margaret (Peggy) Ramsay.

1964   *Entertaining Mr. Sloane* opens at the New Arts Theatre in London on 6 June; that month Orton completes *The Good and Faithful Servant.* On 29 June *Entertaining Mr. Sloane* is transferred to Wyndham's Theatre and on 5 October to Queen's Theatre. From June to December Orton writes *Loot;* on 31 August *The Ruffian on the Stair* airs on the BBC Third Programme.

1965   *Loot* opens at the Arts Theatre, Cambridge, on 1 February and on 11 April at University Theatre, Manchester. Orton makes first visit to Tangier from May to July; from July to September writes *The Erpingham Camp. Entertaining Mr. Sloane* opens at the Lyceum Theater, New York, on 12 October.

1966   Makes second visit to Tangier from May to July. *The Erpingham Camp* airs on Rediffusion Television on 27 June and opens at the Royal Court Theatre on 21 August. *Funeral Games* airs on Yorkshire Television on 25 August. *The Ruffian on the Stair* airs on BBC Radio on 31 August; *Loot* opens at the Jeannetta Cochran Theatre, London, on 27 September and is transferred to the Criterion Theatre on 1 November. In December

Orton begins writing his *Diaries* and *What the Butler Saw;* his mother dies on 26 December.

1967   *Loot* wins awards from *Evening Standard* and *Plays and Players* in January. Orton writes screenplay for the Beatles, *Up Against It*. *The Good and Faithful Servant* opens on 17 March at King's Head Theatre, London, and airs on Rediffusion Television on 6 April. *Crimes of Passion* opens at the Royal Court Theatre (a double-bill stage version of *The Ruffian on the Stair* and *The Erpingham Camp*) on 6 June. The Beatles reject the option for *Up Against It,* and Oscar Lowenstein picks it up. Orton makes third visit to Tangier from May to July and completes *What the Butler Saw* in July. On 9 August is murdered by Halliwell, who takes his own life. Funeral service for Orton is held on 18 August at West Chapel, Golders Green Crematorium (Halliwell's funeral service is held at Enfield, Middlesex), and their ashes are scattered over Golders Green. *Loot* ends run on 25 August after 400 performances.

1968   *Loot* opens 18 March at the Biltmore Theater, New York.

1969   *What the Butler Saw* opens 5 March at the Queen's Theatre, London; *Crimes of Passion* opens 26 October at the Astor Place Theater, New York.

1970   *What the Butler Saw* opens 4 May at the McAlpin Rooftop Theater, New York.

1975   A retrospective Joe Orton season is held at the Royal Court Theatre (*Entertaining Mr. Sloane, Loot,* and *What the Butler Saw*) in June and July.

1978   *Prick Up Your Ears*, a biography of Joe Orton by John Lahr, is published.

1984   In September *Loot* opens at the Lyric Theatre, London, with Leonard Rossiter.

1986   *Loot* opens 18 February at the Manhattan Theater Club, New York, and is transferred to the Music Box Theater on 7 April. John Lahr's dramatic collage *Diary of a Somebody* opens 6 December at the Cottesloe Theatre, London. *Diaries* published.

1987   Lahr's *Diary of a Somebody*, expanded to a full-length play, opens at the King's Head Theatre, London. Film of *Prick Up Your Ears* is released.

1989   *What the Butler Saw* opens 8 March at the Manhattan Theater Club, New York. On 27 July Britain's Homosexual Bill becomes law, decriminalizing consensual homosexuality by adults and establishing 21 as the age of adulthood. Tom Ross's musical stage adaptation of *Up Against It* opens 4 December at the Public Theater, New York.

1994   Britain's legal age for consensual sex is set at 18 on 21 February.

1995   *What the Butler Saw* opens 2 March on the Lyttelton stage of the Royal National Theatre.

Chapter One

A Somebody

Nothing was unusual about Joe Orton's life for his first 17 years. Everything during the remaining 17 years was a wickedly deliberate contradiction of the pattern and values of those early years.

The eldest of four children—one brother and two sisters—John Kingsley Orton was born on 1 January 1933 in Leicester to William and Elsie Kingsley Orton. They moved shortly thereafter to 9 Fayhurst Road, Saffron Lane Estates, Leicester, England. Orton assumed the name of Joe during his London years to avoid confusion with a contemporary, John Osborne, and, according to John Lahr, to shed his image as "failed novelist and acolyte of Kenneth Halliwell."[1]

Biographically convenient, Orton's life divides itself into three distinct periods: the first 17 years spent in Leicester, ending with his moving to London to attend the Royal Academy of Dramatic Arts (RADA); an apprenticeship period of sorts, beginning with his year at RADA (1950) and his living with Kenneth Halliwell, a fellow RADA student, during which time the two collaborated in writing a number of novels, and ending 12 years later with their six-month imprisonment in 1962 for stealing and defacing library books; and the years of Orton's progressively successful public career—1963–67—along with Halliwell's dying hopes for any sort of career and his increasing resentment of Orton's success. Halliwell's visible deterioration ended in his violent murder-suicide of Orton and himself on 9 August 1967.

Orton's father worked as a gardener for the city of Leicester. Frail and cowed, he found in his work a refuge from his wife, a physically large woman, intimidating in her demands that he provide better than he did for their family. The two had met in a pub where, endowed with a reasonably good voice, Elsie Orton would frequently sing. She continued her pub frequenting after her children were born. Regarding her eldest as her most gifted child, she aggressively favored him, even as she misunderstood his talent. One example of this misunderstanding is her enrolling him at a local private business college when he had failed his eleven-plus examinations. He succeeded in learning to take shorthand

1

and to type, but his real interests were the various theatrical groups in Leicester.

There was little emotional warmth in the family, as related by Orton's siblings and most ironically illustrated in Orton's account of his attendance at his mother's funeral in December of 1966. By that time the John Orton who at the age of 16 had chided himself for neglect of all the virtues and achievements that are the mark of respectability—saving, playing tennis, paying for his gramophone—had undergone a complete transformation to Joe Orton, successful dramatist. His metamorphosis involved personal habits such as finding, on his way to his mother's funeral, "a bit of quick sex in a derelict house"[2] and a postfuneral bit after he and Leonie (a sister) had spent the afternoon cleaning out cupboards. Furthermore, he returned to London with his mother's false teeth, shocking the cast of *Loot* with a request that they substitute them for the teeth used in the production.

After Elsie Orton's death, the family placed William in a home for the aged—one that Orton never visited. William, who survived his son, heard the news of Joe Orton's death on a television newscast, not from his family who had been notified by the police, an ironic parallel to the manner in which a few years earlier he had learned of his son's legal troubles for defacing library books.

When Orton put his Leicester life behind him to enter RADA on 1 January 1950, he met a fellow student, Kenneth Halliwell, eight years his senior, who later invited him to share his flat at 161 West End Lane in northwest London, both moving again in 1959 to a new flat Halliwell had purchased at 25 Noel Road in North London's Islington section. Until their deaths in 1967, their lives were inextricably entwined. His relationship with Halliwell was the only lengthy and deeply personal tie in a life whose experiences consisted of an uncommunicative family, prolific and brief sexual encounters, and acquaintances with figures in the theater, particularly his agent, Peggy Ramsay.

Their year at RADA led Orton and Halliwell nowhere, and after Halliwell's money ran out, they subsisted on a weekly government dole of £3 until 1964, when Orton earned a considerable income from his first success. They spent their time reading books borrowed from libraries in Hampstead and Islington. The formally educated Halliwell directed Orton's reading of classical writers—among them, Aristophanes, Lucian, Voltaire—introducing him to a world heretofore denied him. With his grammar school education, Halliwell was teacher, friend, surrogate father, and, in their earlier years, sexual partner to Orton. Orton's own education had left him culturally deprived.

Orton's debt to Halliwell was enormous—until, that is, his education was completed and the security provided by Halliwell was no longer needed. Even before the successes, however, Orton found himself gradually weaned from Halliwell's influence. Together they had written a number of novels that were never published: *The Silver Bucket, The Mechanical Womb, The Last Days of Sodom, The Boy Hairdresser*. It became increasingly evident to both that Halliwell had none of Orton's writing talent or driving creative energy. Halliwell resigned himself to his limitations after a publisher's rejection of his solo novel, *Priapus in the Shrubbery* (1959). Eventually he concentrated on collage painting, but, as with his writing, his talent here was minimal. Even as both men had rapidly become nobodies in their first 10 years or so together, Orton was growing into the somebody he longed to be, whereas Halliwell remained in place.

Public recognition, denied them heretofore, suddenly arrived in a perverse form, a six-month prison sentence for stealing and defacing library books. During a four-year period, 1959–62, they had furtively smuggled books in and out of libraries, returning them enriched with pictorial and verbal embellishments. Then, positioned in corners of the library, they watched readers react. Orton found it "very funny, very interesting."[3]

Their mischief consisted of removing 1,653 plates from art books and inserting blurbs, drawings, and paste-ups on jackets and book pages—some of them obscene. The more spicy defacings included the pasting of a female nude over the picture of the author of a book on etiquette, a drawing of Dame Sybil Thorndyke locked in a cell and accompanied by a caption regarding her sexual services for American G.I.s, and a piece of literary criticism in a Peter Wimsey story by Dorothy Sayers. One drawing that British newspapers reproduced was that of a monkey's head on a rose on the cover of a gardening book. Lahr records the ironic detail of Orton's father, who, expecting to read an article on gardening, instead read of his son's arrest.

After several years of amusing themselves in this fashion, Orton and Halliwell were caught in a sting operation conducted by library staff—one that Orton would have prided himself on had he not been its victim. Both were arrested, tried, and sentenced in 1962 to six months in prison, at first in Wormwood Scrubs and then in transfers to separate prisons.

For Halliwell, the experience was humiliating, but for Orton creative energies were unleashed, and in the next year success, long elusive, was his.

In 1963 he acquired a literary agent, Peggy Ramsay, sold *The Ruffian on the Stair* to the BBC Third Programme, and wrote *Entertaining Mr. Sloane*. In 1964, a year of prolific activity, the BBC aired *The Ruffian on the Stair* (31 August), *Entertaining Mr. Sloane* was successfully produced, and Orton not only completed the writing of *The Good and Faithful Servant* but also wrote *Loot*. These successes, however, were followed in 1965 by frustrations caused by failed out-of-town tryouts of *Loot* and a disastrous American premiere of *Entertaining Mr. Sloane*. But Orton's first trip to Tangier and his completion of *The Erpingham Camp* were consolatory. With a new cast and director in 1966, *Loot* began a long critically and commercially successful London run, earning best-play awards from both the *Evening Standard* and *Plays and Players* and then moving, with financial help from Terence Rattigan, from the small Arts Theatre to the West End's Criterion Theatre.

With his successes in London and his holidays in Tangier, the next three years (1964–67) were for Orton a time of recognition and personal satisfaction. He had become a somebody. In December 1966 he was secure enough to act on the repeated urging of his agent to keep a diary, and so the boyhood diary (discontinued in 1950 and to date unpublished) was resumed, this time with a style and substance that contrasted outrageously with those of the diary of his early years. At the time of his death he had completed the writing of his third and last long play, *What the Butler Saw*.

The most extraordinary fact about Orton is that in just four years of his prematurely shortened life he had established a reputation on the basis of three long stage plays and four short radio/television plays. Since his death that reputation has grown and earned him a place in English dramatic history. His name is linked with those of William Congreve, Ben Jonson, Oscar Wilde, and George Bernard Shaw. In the same year (1966) that Ronald Bryden had called world attention to Tom Stoppard's *Rosencrantz and Guildenstern Are Dead* in its production at the Edinburgh Festival, he reviewed *Loot*, asserting that the play had established "Orton's niche in English Drama" and dubbing Orton "the Oscar Wilde of Welfare State Gentility,"[4] a soubriquet that has stuck to Orton as has no other. Terence Rattigan praised *Entertaining Mr. Sloane* for its classic construction and appreciated its style "that could be compared with Restoration comedies. I saw Congreve in it. I saw Wilde. To me, in some ways it was better than Wilde because it had more bite" (168). Rattigan spoke with action as well as with words by providing £3,000 to have the play moved to the larger Criterion Theatre.

Extraordinary as well is the inseparability of Orton's life and work from that of Halliwell who—more educated, articulate, and intellectual than Orton—was the driving force in filling in the huge gaps in Orton's literary education. Halliwell's education of Orton, both in the recommendation of readings and their jointly written novels, was necessary until their months in prison during which Orton developed a creative detachment that was increasingly felt and resented by Halliwell. Yet Orton remained loyal, even to their final days when Halliwell's worsening mental state had become increasingly the concern of their acquaintances. Halliwell's influence is seen not only in Orton's reference to *Entertaining Mr. Sloane* as "our play" but also to his public acknowledgment of Halliwell's providing him with titles, the most important being that for *Loot*. Orton's loyalty is seen in his helping Halliwell deliver his collages to an art dealer even as Orton was planning separate living arrangements. Ironically, the plans were never realized.

A third extraordinary event in the life and career of Orton was his decision to act on the urging of his agent, Peggy Ramsay, to keep a diary. Orton's *Diaries* are not only a key to his work but also, in and of themselves, a memoir of literary significance. In them he flaunts his defiance of a repressive society, frank in his views of his family, Halliwell, acquaintances, other writers, and his own works. As in his plays, the metaphor for his defiance is the phallus, and his secret adventures in English public lavatories and openly homosexual life in Tangier are recorded with a highly detailed, detached comic skill. Like Ramsay, who was hesitant to sell *Entertaining Mr. Sloane* for fear of being accused of its being Pinterish, Orton was also hesitant at first to act on Ramsay's suggestion, fearing that his diary could not possibly be published. Then with a self-confidence gained from his successes, he began it in December 1966.

Adding to the unusual nature of Orton's career is the spectacular contribution to Orton scholarship by an American, John Lahr, son of one of the most famous of American farce actors of the twentieth century, Bert Lahr. Having learned of the existence of Orton's diaries in 1970, John Lahr published the biography *Prick Up Your Years* in 1978 and then edited the *Diaries* in 1986. In addition he wrote a play, *Diary of a Somebody*, whose words are drawn from the *Diaries*, introductions to editions of Orton's work, and, of course, reviews of Orton's plays. Lahr's scholarship has some of the inseparability from Orton's name, as Halliwell's life has from Orton's. He edited the *Diaries* with special care to avoid hurting or embarrassing Orton's living relatives and acquaintances. Lahr, having grown up with the art of the farceur, was superbly qualified to undertake not only the exhaustive editing but also the analysis and evaluation of the nature and techniques of farce. With his background, he understood and was able to articulate the dominant role of misrule in comedy—one in evidence from its earliest Aristophanic and Plautine manifestations.

As a record of the last eight months of his life, the events recorded in his diary vividly unify Orton's life, melding the personal and professional, private and public, involved and detached realities of an artist's life with an inextricability that is a biographer's dream. Although the title page of *The Orton Diaries* was not returned to the Orton estate after the inquest into Orton's death, the coroner listed the title *Diary of a Somebody* in his official report. The events and achievements of Orton's short life are a testament of his attempt to be a somebody. Nowhere is that testament more flagrantly and more outrageously demonstrated than in the *Diaries*.

Everything in the *Diaries* portrays a personal life scandalously opposite his working-class upbringing by a mother with middle-class pretensions and a father who loved his family but was unable to make emotional connections with them. Elsie Orton worked as a machine operator in the hosiery factories of Leicester. William Orton was a gardener for the city of Leicester, never realizing his dream of having his own greenhouse. Feeling failure even at being a good gardener, he nevertheless invested his job with the attention his family never received. His son's destiny, however, was not to be satisfied with being a nobody.

For years Orton increasingly engaged in attempts to escape the banalities of the middle-class aspirations of his mother, the emotional deprivation of a dysfunctional family, and the cultural desert of his upbringing. Escape in his early years consisted of involvement with various theatrical groups in Leicester, and his final break with his stultifying family and his even more stultifying job as office clerk occurred on his seventeenth birthday, 1 January 1950, when he left Leicester for London and the RADA. The break was his ticket to freedom, fame, and, ironically, to another prison of sorts in his relationship with Halliwell—a relationship from which his plans to escape came too late and ended in his violent death.

His insistence on becoming a somebody and having his own voice is seen in his distancing himself from two famous contemporaries, Rattigan and Pinter, whose encouragement early on was crucial to Orton's reputation. Rattigan had written Orton regarding *Sloane*, "I don't think you've written a masterpiece. But I think you have written the most exciting and stimulating first play . . . that I've seen in thirty years of play-going" (*Diaries*, 114). About *Loot* Rattigan congratulated Orton on writing "the best second play I have read in fifty years. . . . It is so good that I hate you almost as much as I love you" (*Diaries*, 114).

Pinter, writing to Orton to explain his criticism of *Loot*, also admired Orton's plays for their "remarkable balance . . . they're many layered things. The great distinction and joy of your best writing is that (within a beautifully organized rhythmic structure) it possesses an inner resonance of shifting references *and* at the same time a sustained sense of dramatic momentum from one sentence to the next (I don't apologize for that sentence)" (Lahr 1978, 286).

But encouragement from two important but very different playwrights—one a highly successful practitioner of traditional plays and the other a current leader of the stage avant-garde—only evoked an honest apology from Orton for not being able to return Rattigan's compliment and an attempt to separate himself stylistically from Pinter—much as he admired him—which we see in his notes to the Royal Court Theatre in regard to the production of *The Ruffian on the Stair*: "The play mustn't be presented as an example of the now out-dated 'mystery' school—*Vide* early Pinter. Everything is as clear as the most reactionary *Telegraph* reader could wish. There is a beginning, a middle, and an end" (Lahr 1978, 130). Orton's directions continue with references to the pauses for which Pinter had become famous: "The play must be directed without long significant pauses. Any pauses must be natural pauses" (Lahr 1978, 130, 131).

Independent even of peer admirers such as Rattigan and Pinter, Orton could no longer ignore his need for independence from Halliwell. Their living together in a one-room flat for 16 years, Halliwell's tutoring of Orton, and their collaborative writing of unpublished novels had all served their purpose. More to the point, Halliwell's own sense of failure and his increasingly irrational demands on Orton had reached psychopathic proportions. Like the experience of Joyce's Stephen Dedalus, Orton felt he must flee the nets that would hold him. His tragedy is that he waited too long to do so. When he began planning for separate living arrangements for himself and Halliwell, the latter's psychopathy had reached a flash point.

On 9 August 1967 Orton was scheduled to meet with Richard Lester at Twickenham Studios to discuss the film script Orton had written for the Beatles—*Up Against It*—and Halliwell had an appointment with a psychiatrist at St. Bernard's Hospital the next day. Neither man kept his appointment, for that night Halliwell bludgeoned Orton to death with a hammer and then committed suicide with an overdose of nembuttal pills. Halliwell's fatal blows to Orton's head were the result of what, in retrospect, were both unheeded warnings to Orton and behavioral pleas for help by Halliwell. Their sexual relationship had long since changed to one of housekeeping and to Orton's increasing need of sexual and artistic satisfaction elsewhere. Their arguments on many matters, inflamed by Orton's success, became more frequent, resulting in Halliwell's physical attack of Orton in Tangier after Orton's visit to a boyfriend. In retrospect, this incident seems a rehearsal for the fatal attack of 9 August.

After their return to London from their last Tangier vacation, Orton begins his last entry in *The Orton Diaries*, 1 August 1967, "Said goodbye to Kenneth this morning. He seemed odd. On the spur of the moment I asked if he wanted to come home to Leicester with me. He looked surprised and said, No" (*Diaries*, 265).

At Orwell's funeral poetic tributes were made: Harold Pinter read Marion Lochhead's "Non Est Perpetua," and Donald Pleasance read his "Hilarium Memoriam J.O." As one reads Lahr's description of Orton's funeral service at Golders Green Crematorium (Lahr 1978, 278–79), the ritual, which was grist for Orton's farcical mill during his life, is as somberly incongruous as the sentiments uttered in his farces, even to the response of Douglas Orton (a brother) to Peggy Ramsay's suggestion that Orton's and Halliwell's ashes be mixed: "'Well,' he said, agreeing, 'as long as nobody hears about it in Leicester'" (Lahr 1978, 279). It is the kind of line that Orton consistently lifted from life for his farcical art.

Orton's stage life continued posthumously in the failed production of his last play, *What the Butler Saw* (1969), with audiences nearly booing Ralph Richardson off the stage. As Orton himself might have expected, the Mrs. Edna Welthorpes would be as obstreperous in their objections to this play as they were to *Entertaining Mr. Sloane* and *Loot*. What was unexpected, however, was the critics' failure to realize the difference between the play as produced and the play as written. Successive productions and literary analyses have proved the critics wrong.

Orton's novel *Head to Toe* was published in 1971, and at the time of his death he was planning to write a play, tentatively titled *Prick Up Your Ears*, "a historical farce set on the eve of Edward VII's coronation in 1902" (Lahr 1978, 22).

It is this title that Lahr picked up for his biography. His exhaustively detailed account of Orton's life includes interviews with members of Orton's immediate family and also with teachers, members of provincial theater groups with whom Orton was associated as a youth, and figures of the London theater. Lahr was granted access to letters, diaries, and papers of the Orton estate. Lahr followed the biography with his edition of the *Diaries*, including valuable introductory commentary. He also wrote the introductions to *What the Butler Saw* and to Orton's *Complete Plays*. He picked up yet another title from Orton, this one for a play about the last eight months of Orton's life—*Diary of a Somebody*, Orton's early choice of a title for his *Diaries*. Lahr wrote the play, produced at the Kings' Head, a small pub theater in North London, in collaboration with its director, Jonathan Myerson. Lahr was also involved in the film *Prick Up Your Ears*, based on Lahr's biography, written by Alan Bennett and directed by Stephen Frears.

In a long spate of letter-writing under various aliases, Orton took on the hypocrisies of corporations, churches, libraries, and, of course, the middle-class theater audience. Mrs. Edna Welthorpe is the alias with which he flaunted critics as well as the average, middle-class theatergoer. Through her, he supported the negative critics, even outdoing them in her moral denunciation of his plays. On some occasions he followed a Welthorpe letter with one from a Donald A. Hartley, who approved of Orton's plays so much that he planned to see a given play a second or third time.

A curious phenomenon attendant on Orton's Mrs. Edna Welthorpe is an earlier version, an Aunt Edna created by Rattigan as a defense against the critics who berated him for writing well-made plays for middle-class audiences rather than plays with ideas. Rattigan wrote a play about a fictional trial in which he defends his plays by defending his middle-class audience in the person of Aunt Edna. She goes to the theater for "laughter, tears and excitement. . . . She is bored by propaganda, enraged at being 'alienated,' loathes placards coming down and telling her what is going to happen next, hates a lot of philosophical talk on the stage with nothing happening at all, enjoys poetry only when it is dramatic and fine prose only when there is action to go with it. Her greatest joy is still and always will be for a good strong meaty plot told by good strong meaty characters."[5] His play followed a debate he initiated on the play of ideas in the *New Statesman* on 4 March 1950. The debate was joined by contemporaries Benn Levy, James Bridie, Sean O'Casey, Christopher Fry, and Shaw himself. Having written his major plays in earlier decades when deviation from sexual norms had to be disguised in heterosexual terms, Rattigan, although publicly applauding Orton's work for its construction and style, must have welcomed the honesty of the younger playwright's work as well as what he described as a strong meaty plot told by strong meaty characters, for Orton's plots and characters are certainly that.

The much abused Edna enjoys yet a third incarnation in Dame Edna Everage, Barrie Humphries's television persona, famous for her hideously and hilariously vulgar middle-class taste. Unlike Rattigan's Aunt Edna and Orton's Mrs. Edna Welthorpe, Dame Edna Everage is resplendent in her vulgarity. As a housewife/superstar, she revels in her contradictions—"hilarious and malign, polite and lewd, generous and envious, high and low comic."[6]

Humphries shares a biographer—Lahr—with Orton. Lahr's *Dame Edna Everage and the Rise of Western Civilization* (1992) has an Ortonesque quality. In his tribute to Humphries in the Preface, Lahr—the recipient of "certain privileges" by virtue of having been raised in the household of a famous clown—associates Humphries with the great clowns of his own father's time: Buster Keaton, Groucho Marx, and Eddy Foy. He speaks of the "grief behind the zaniness of the mutant breed so articulately defended by Thomas Mann in *The Confessions of Felix Krull* as 'exceptions, side-splitting world-renouncing monks of unreason, cavorting hybrids, part human and part insane art'" (Lahr 1992, xi). These are the Lords of Misrule, a term Lahr repeatedly applies to Orton and to all great clowns. Orton's acts of unreason—letter-writing, book defacing, sexual larks in men's lavatories—might well subscribe to Lahr's description of the distinctions of the clown. In his plays Orton has contained and shaped the perverse cavorting of the clown within the conventions of the well-made play.

Chapter Two

Orton as Trickster

"I shall just do all my box of tricks," wrote Orton on 16 January 1967 (*Diaries*, 66). The context for his remark was a request by the Beatles' management for a film script from Orton. Orton's reaction to the request was to do a "Sloane and Hal on them [the audience]," a risk slight enough since "nobody who sees the film will have seen *Sloane* or *Loot*" (66). The trick eventually focused on Orton's decision to go back to his then unpublished novel, published posthumously as *Head to Toe*. One of Orton's literary tricks was a consistent reworking of the characters and situations of his early unpublished writings. *The Ruffian on the Stair* is derived from *The Boy Hairdresser*. The minor works *Up Against It* and *Until She Screams*—both sexually suggestive titles—are derivations of *Head to Toe* and *The Patient Dowager*, respectively. As characters, Hal and Dennis in *Loot* are patterned after Donnelly and Peterson in *The Boy Hairdresser*. Orton's tricks run the gamut, from those in his personal life that led to his imprisonment to those that are a part of his literary style.

Among the major motifs that run through Lahr's biography of Orton, *Prick Up Your Ears*, is that of the farceur as clown-trickster—the lord of misrule and the master of disguise who entertains his audience as he flaunts them with their own hypocrisies. The clown defines his peculiar identity by carefully chosen disguises and tricks with which he celebrates his anarchical impulses. He establishes his persona by means of a symbolic object, such as the cane of Charlie Chaplin or, as with Aristophanes in *Lysistrata*, the collective symbols of battering rams, fires, pots of water, feminine wiles, or pretended pregnancies—all of which constitute phallic clowning about war and peace.

No less than the farcical art of his predecessors, Orton's tricks have roots in nature's most forceful celebrant of freedom—the phallus. In the final scene of his last stage play he flaunts in the audience's face the offending organ from a bombed statue of Sir Winston Churchill. Even the admired actor, Sir Ralph Richardson, was offended, so that in the failed original production of *What the Butler Saw* (1969) he, along with the censor, insisted that a cigar be substituted for the phallus. In the published version the revised ending was included as an alternate. Orton was no longer alive to protest, but in a 1975 production at the Royal Court Theatre the phallus was restored. Orton would have enjoyed a revengeful satisfaction at its restoration. A cunning dramatic trick, the phallus in the farce is Orton's farewell embodiment of a series of tricks he had so gleefully perpetrated on authorities during his short life.

Orton's bag of tricks includes the many aliases he assumed in public correspondence, the defacings of library books that earned him a six-month prison term, and, especially, the careful keeping of a diary for nearly eight months before he was murdered. In his diary he recorded in detail the conversations he overheard on public transportation and among the neighbors in his apartment building, his sexual adventures, and his attitudes toward other writers, which he recorded with his usual total honesty, even at the expense of his famous admirers, like Rattigan and Pinter. The sexual inuendos and shenanigans in his plays reflect the clowning in his personal life, that of the farceur-trickster whose only means of fighting hypocrisy is on its own terms—throwing back at society its own contradictory behavior and language. He has no equal among his contemporaries in this regard.

The same spirit embodied in his daring reinvention of middle-class language is seen in the anarchic behavior of his characters, all guilty of criminality of one sort or another. Anarchy, particularly sexual anarchy, is the rule in his sometimes sophomoric behavior preceding his stage successes and in the transformation of personal pranks into wickedly fascinating accounts in his diaries at the height of his success. There is a chronological continuity to his impishly outrageous pranks. They are a progressive revelation of the growth of a nobody into a farcical artist who commanded the admiration of the best of his contemporaries on the stage. *The Orton Diaries*, concluded only a few days before his death, combine the clowning of his earlier years with the detachment that characterizes his plays. As such, they are an essential account of Orton's writing habits and represent his masterful observation of language and behavior.

Orton's public joking began, appropriately, with teasing letters to such bastions of contemporary culture as the church and commercial institutions. They are some of the same authorities that come under heavy fire in his plays. The letters were written under various aliases, but primarily that of Mrs. Edna Welthorpe, Orton's representative of the taste of "welfare state gentility." The second group of pranks considered here—the book defacements—proved both a curse and a blessing, for it was during his six-month jail term that he claims to have developed the artistic detachment that enabled him to write so much in so few years. The newly acquired discipline was Orton's means of shaping his anarchical instincts, his keen observations of life, and the literary education provided by Halliwell into farcical art. His three long and four short plays give form to the unshaped rebellion of his early years and earned for him stature as an important dramatist of the 1960s. His early tricks developed into serious farces with a stylistic signature unmatched by any of his contemporaries.

Epistolary Surrogates

The first of Orton's tricks to be considered here is his rash of parodic letters concerning sundry matters from food to churches and then later joining in on the public debate about the morality of the successful West End productions of *Entertaining Mr. Sloane* and *Loot.* Even after his stage successes he used Mrs. Edna Welthorpe as his alias persona to express middle-class taste in theater, just as she had earlier demanded certain rights from the public sector on other matters. Orton then balanced off Mrs. Edna Welthorpe with viewers such as John A. Carlsen and Donald H. Hartley, who, respectively, contradicted her opinions with claims to less blinkered views of *Entertaining Mr. Sloane* and with assurances of attending the production for a third time (*Diaries*, 284). Other names assumed by Orton—Peter Pinnell, Jay Chakiris, Alan Crosby, and J. P. H. Joy—not only reflected the audience furor directed at the play but actually joined in with real-life critics like W. A. Darlington of the *Daily Telegraph*, whose reaction was that of "snakes . . . writhing about his feet."[1] Orton's Pinnell picked up Darlington's distaste and his desire for some "fresh, wholesome Leicester Square air" (*Diaries*, 283). Darlington, who modified his views upon a second viewing, admitted to being "held throughout," despite the "shameless and repulsive characters" (Lahr 1978, 170).

Mrs. Edna Welthorpe sympathized with both Darlington and Pinnell and hoped that "ordinary decent people will shortly strike back" (*Diaries*, 283). "Plunged into the dumps for weeks after she had seen his *Entertaining Mr. Sloane*" (*Diaries*, 287), she and her young niece fled from the theater during the intermission of *Loot.* She agreed with the real-life novelist, David Benedictus, who had objected to the awarding of best play designation of *Loot* by the *Evening Standard* and *Plays and Players.*

Orton had preceded her letter with one from Hartley, defending the award.

The harshest public criticism came from powerful figures in the theater world, such as Peter Cadbury and Emile Littler, one the head of the Keith Prowse ticket agency and the other a producer, who denounced the play as "unnaceptable" and "filthy" (Lahr 1978, 172). Left-handedly, however, they actually complimented Orton by associating his play with the "dirty" fare of a National Theatre season that included critically acclaimed productions of Weiss's *Marat/Sade*, Beckett's *Endgame*, and Rudkin's *Afore Night Come*. Clashing with Darlington, Cadbury, and Littler, were Rattigan and Pinter, who wrote Orton admiring letters, and heavyweight authors/critics such as the *Evening Standard*'s John Mortimer, the *Sunday Telegraph*'s Alan Brien, and the usually traditional Harold Hobson of the *Sunday Times*. Orton especially enjoyed Hobson's comparing *Entertaining Mr. Sloane* with Jane Austen's *Northanger Abbey* (Lahr 1978, 167).

As the furor continued, Orton not only had fun in continuing the debates with his entries, pro and con, but he used his journalistic aliases as opportunities to express views dramatized in the plays. Hartley, for example, found the play an oasis in a wasteland, and he enjoyed its exotic landscape with its differing customs "from our own—what else is foreign travel for?" (*Diaries*, 285). In *The Diaries* Orton lashes out at Britain's antisodomy laws, referring to his own preference for younger boys as a custom in Tangier and regarded as rape in England. Another alias, Crosby, picked up on Orton's self-description of being from the gutter. In Crosby's praise of Orton's brilliant dialogue, breath-taking comedy, satisfying drama, and generally well-written play, he exhorted Orton to heed Wilde's comment that "some of us are walking in the gutter, but we can look at the stars" (*Diaries*, 286).

The last two of Orton's trick letters published in his *Diaries* were sent to the Criterion Theatre, to which *Loot* had been transferred with the financial help of Terence Rattigan. One, from J. P. H. Joy, dated 9 April 1967, threatened a complaint to the Lord Chamberlain, and the second, from Mrs. Edna Welthorpe on 14 April, asked Joy to join her in arranging a meeting with the Lord Chamberlain. The joke here is Orton's own delight in the irony of the censor's objection to minor heterosexual material while ignoring the overtly homosexual nature of the play.

The public debate, uniting real and fictional critics, occurred in 1967 in connection with Orton's two successful West End productions. But they have their roots in his earlier letter-writing quarrels during the

1950s. His views of corporate influence dramatized in *The Good and Faithful Servant*, for example, have origins in a series of letters from Mrs. Edna Welthorpe to *The National Trade Press Ltd.*, requesting 78 tickets to an International Trade Fashion Fair, later chiding them for their mistaking of her request for only seven or eight, finally receiving satisfaction with an explanation as well as the eight tickets requested. In another spate of letters Edna, threatening a lawsuit, took on the mail-order firm of Littlewoods about a matter of catalogs. In still another she taunted a food concern, Smedley's Limited, for the edible starch and locust bean gum ingredients rather than more raspberry content.

Her interest in the theater began in the 1950s with a letter to the Heath Street Baptist Church, requesting the use of a hall for a three-performance production of a play entitled *The Pansy*. She appealed to the church's sense of tolerance for homosexuality. The minister's delay in replying evoked increasingly rude responses, one of these irately accusing the minister of avoiding a controversial issue. He wrote her that if the decision were left to him, he would have to reject the request. At end the series Edna's niece (also her successor as secretary to the Phallus Players) informed the clergyman of her aunt's death.

Illegal Acts

The most notorious component in Orton's bag of tricks was his and Halliwell's stealing of library books and returning them secretly, fancifully "emended" with drawings, frequently of a sexual nature. Methods used by librarians such as trying to catch the culprits red-handed or to trace their identities by handwriting proved unsuccessful. Finally, Sidney Porrett, a legal clerk of the Borough of Islington, turned the tables on Orton and Halliwell in the guise of an inquiry about an abandoned car in Noel Road. To the satisfaction of the authorities, the typeface of a reply by Halliwell matched that in the defacings of the books, and both Halliwell, who repented, and the "victimized" Orton, who did not, were sentenced to six-month jail terms. After reprimanding Porrett for the letter trick, Orton was reminded by Porrett that he was only sinking to Orton's level, at the same time keeping one step ahead of Orton and Halliwell. Orton especially resented the attempts of Islington authorities to get at his and Halliwell's savings and called them hounds of vengeance for the book-damage fee he and Halliwell had to pay—a reduced amount of £262. Orton's source for the the detection logic and maneuvering of Sergeant Truscott in *Loot* is the treatment he received at the hands of legal authorities. Unrepentant, he especially attacked the threatening nature of the law in Truscott's merciless attack on Hal even when the latter was down. Having beaten him, Truscott then identified himself as the higher authority to which Hal said he wished to appeal.

Their criminal acts—jokes to Orton and Halliwell—especially irritated authorities because of the highly detailed style, which was proof that the defacements had been executed with extraordinary "care and intelligence." One magistrate, voicing an ironic truth, saw the jokes as the work of frustrated authors. However scandalous, the defacings had their own artistically satirical flair. On a gardening book, for example, Orton said that he had "stuck" a "monkey's face in the middle of a rose. It was a very beautiful rose." He pasted on the cover of a book on etiquette a picture of a female nude. He wrote "false blurbs on the inside of Gollancz' books" with their convenient blank flaps and inserted his own literary criticism, particularly in the Peter Wimsey stories by Dorothy Sayers. Orton's and Halliwell's lack of respect for hallowed literary figures alienated the court—for instance, the Arden editions of Shakespeare, on whose *Titus Andronicus* was imposed a copy of Goya's *Saturn Devouring Her Children*. Heads of birds, monkeys, and cats grotesquely adorned the books, frequently replacing the heads of respected individuals.

In one pasting that evokes Orton's use of the Churchillian phallus in *What the Butler Saw*, Sybil Thorndyke, one of England's most highly respected actresses, is seen "staring at the mammoth genitalia of a superimposed Greek torso" (Lahr 1978, 81). Orton admitted to his and Halliwell's furtive enjoyment of watching library users reading the "enriched" books just returned to the library. The library, as Lahr notes, had become Orton's and Halliwell's theater as they were entertained by the reactions to their productions.

Lahr calls attention to an interesting reference to book stealing in their joint (unpublished) autobiographical novel, *The Boy Hairdresser*. Their fictional egos, Peterson and Donnelly, explain their acts as a reaction to what they see as civilization's misrepresentation: the holding "carrots in the air to make donkeys work. Do you know what it wants in exchange for a house, a car, a larger house, two cars, a television in every room?" (Lahr 1978, 84). The image here is a resentful contrast with the spartan one-room flat in which the two men lived until their deaths.

The flagrant crossing of legal boundaries was damaging to Halliwell's pride, but for Orton the crimes became a means to channel his hurt into a five-year burst of writing.

Oh, Calcutta!

The most raffish of Orton's short pieces is his unrelievedly porno-graphic piece, *Until She Screams*, submitted in response to a request from Kenneth Tynan for his revue *Oh, Calcutta!* The request was for "a sketch to do with sex." Because he thought that his contribution would be "doomed from the start," he decided not to "put myself out," and so he went back to a piece he had written sometime around 1960—before his prison term—entitled "The Patient Dowager." He finished the typing of the skit on 24 February 1967, after slightly altering "some of the more deliberately pornographic element." The average audience, however, might find it difficult to imagine anything less deliberately pornographic. Tynan had asked that it "be straightfor-ward, and no 'artistic' shit" (*Diaries*, 90–91), and Orton accommodat-ed.

Involving one of Orton's favorite themes, sexual sharing, the sketch is about the sexual indulgences of an upper-class family consisting of the Dowager, Lady Shane (Eliza), her niece and nephew-in-law, Laura and Charles Terrington, and their daughter Lesbia. The conversation on this day in the Morning Room of Shane Abbey concerns Lesbia, who is fast asleep after arriving home at 3 A.M. The sexual act is immediately intro-duced in Laura's complaint that "Lesbia and Myra Ticklesand are getting 'it' too often."[2] Lady Shane is reminded that she can't get "it" often enough, and with her complaint, Orton begins an imaginative series of induced sexual encounters involving the satisfaction of Lady Shane by Charles and Laura by the butler, O'Dwyer. The two main episodes are conducted behind a "rare Chinese screen, hand-painted with glorious representations of waterbirds in flight" (*Screams*, 52). Amid Lady Shane's exclamations of satisfaction "the strains of the Anvil Chorus from the immortal Verdi's 'Il Trovatore' are heard," and she and Charles are "fin-ished" just as the chorus finishes. Having complained of "stuck" reels of embroidery cotton and needles with which she had attempted satisfac-tion she could not receive from Charles, Laura is relieved by the butler, whose radioactive member—the result of a nuclear accident at an atom-ic center at which he had worked—is able to retrieve cotton, pins, and thread.

Orton's phallus-flaunting is consistently farcical throughout, the dialogue and actions conducted as a matter of daily routine as ordinary as the traditional family breakfast in which food and other such mat-ters are the topics of conversation. Orton builds the incidents slowly, each one more outrageous than its predecessor. Among them is the use of rolled-up magazines and periodicals, which are not very pliant, as Lady Shane complains. Like the music attendant on Eliza's satisfaction, the strains of Tchaikovsky's *1812 Overture* are heard during Laura's assignation with the butler. What seems like one climactic action only leading to another culminates in the appearance of the very upset and frightened Lesbia, who has just been fighting off the advances of her great-aunt and who now discovers her mother with the butler. Tearfully she bursts out with her fear of growing up unbalanced and of being given a complex.

O'Dwyer is the only butler in the plays of Orton, and the sketch might well be entitled *What the Butler Did*. The elders of the family in their bizarre sexual activity contrast with Lesbia, and they have distant echoes of the madness in *What the Butler Saw*. Orton cleverly stages the action in the context of the best of the civilized world—classical music, priceless Renaissance portraits, and an old English house with its rare period furniture. Having integrated low life and high comedy in the lower-middle classes in most of his plays, Orton takes special delight in according the upper class the same treatment. Mixing pornography with high art, however, he does not make one into the other as he does in his full-length stage plays.

As another element in Orton's bag of tricks, *Until She Screams* echoes with a number of Orton's hallmarks found in his major plays. There is the sexual sharing among the family members as in *Entertaining Mr. Sloane* and *What the Butler Saw*. There are the innocents, the pair of Lesbia and Myra, like the closely knit brothers in *The Ruffian on the Stair*, Hal and Dennis in *Loot*, the twins in *The Good and Faithful Servant*, and Geraldine and Nick in *What the Butler Saw*. One can see a slight resemblance between the smoke emanating from under Lady Shane's expensive gown and the butler's readioactive phallus with the "blaze from above" that gilds the appearance of Sergeant Match, in leopard-skin dress, at the end of *What the Butler Saw*. The skit, however, contains a real butler whose seeing is no matter of importance but whose doing resolves problems for the family.

Orton's sexual caricature knows no bounds, human or artistic. One is aware from the start that each episode will only outdo its predecessor for shock value, and this predictability has the effect of making the sketch what Tynan asked that it be—straightforward without any consideration of art.

The Orton Diaries

It is in his *Diaries* that Orton's serious tricksterism reveals the essential man and writer. They deserve a place among the notable diaries of the past for their insights into both the style and subject matter of Orton's plays. In them he exhibits, without benefit of artistic shaping, what Penelope Gilliatt has described as his "cold, marvellous, funny fury" (*Diaries*, 17), the driving force in his attempt to be somebody. With success his, he acquiesced finally to persistent prodding from his agent, Peggy Ramsay, to keep a diary of his adventures in Tangier, where he found the necessary sexual freedom not only from societal stereotyping but also from potential illegality. An account of the last seven months of his life, the diaries begin on 20 December 1966. Originally titled by Orton *Diary of a Somebody*, they became, in Lahr's scrupulous edition, *The Orton Diaries* (1986). If the *Diaries* are Orton's farewell, so their publication, according to Lahr himself, is Lahr's farewell to a scholarly endeavor that began in 1970 and is of a longer duration, in fact, than Halliwell's own life with Orton.

With the honesty that characterized his life and his work, Orton writes freely of his private sex life conducted naturally in Tangier and furtively in men's lavatories in England. Shocking to the Edna Welthorpes of the world, the accounts in their frank, matter-of-fact style are at outlandishly delightful odds with the subject, resulting in a form of diary art that its, perhaps, unprecedented. They seem unintended as a revenge trick, as do Orton's pseudonymous letters and book defacements. Similarly, the intention to offend, about which he frequently spoke in connection with his plays, is gone, and in its place is the assured, plain-dealing style whose effect is, at times, as funny as that of his plays. Shaped and seasoned by five years of successful writing, the *Diaries* are sometimes short play dialogues and at other times narratives—all detached in style and linked by the same Ortonesque tone of his plays. Like his plays, there is the wit that unself-consciously dislocates expectations and prevailing assumptions. The double binds in which he often found himself and of which he has spoken have vanished, except for his situation with Halliwell. The voice in the *Diaries* is the mature Joe Orton at his best.

In the early entries Orton introduces a few motifs that continue throughout. One of these is his recording of conversations with neighbors in his apartment building, particularly Mr. and Mrs. Corden and

Miss Boynes—the latter evidently on terms of hostile neighborliness to the Cordens. They are, like his mother, the kind of welfare-state gentility from which Orton drew a Mr. McLeavy and a Kath. Orton frequently converses with them, as in his complimenting Mrs. Corden on her dress worn to a party given by her husband's firm. When she proudly confesses that the material for the dress had come all the way from Africa, Orton remarks to himself, "I wasn't surprised. She looked like a f—— hottentot in it" (*Diaries*, 38). The situation of Miss Boynes is ironically appropriate, for one of her continual topics of conversation is her intention to move away from her irritating neighbors—the Cordens. Eventually she does move, and, in retrospect, her progress toward that move ironically parallels Orton's own growing desire to move from the tiny one-room flat and from Halliwell himself.

Orton's ear for conversational idiom, much like that of his own mother or of Kath in *Entertaining Mr. Sloane*, is seen in a meeting with Miss Boynes during the Christmas season. Full of the Christmas spirit, she proclaims the Cordens "the filthiest people she'd ever met. She said, 'I had to do Mrs. Corden's hair for her attendance [at an annual Christmas party] at the Savoy. And you know I can't stand touching other people's hair. But I did it for goodwill. And I pressed her dress because my board is more suitable. But when she hinted that I do Mr. Corden's suit as well, I nearly took off.'" The conversation continues with additional insults regarding Mrs. Corden's new fur hat. With a toss of her head, she admits to being put out by it. Orton asks whether it was "'out of the box.' Because Mrs. C. has boxes and cupboards full of rubbish. 'Oh, no!' said Miss Boynes. It was the latest thing." Laughing to himself after she leaves, Orton records, "If she could see herself as others see her" (*Diaries*, 39).

The fascination of this diary trick of Orton's is that routinely dull conversations such as these on a day in which nothing else much happened are dramatic contrasts with the scandalous details of his Tangier holidays or his visit to the home of the Beatles. A detached account of his mother's funeral is eclipsed by his narration of two sexual encounters in men's lavatories, one before and the other after the dreary funeral rites. He continued to record observations of banalities along with socially shocking experiences even after his initial stage successes. One kept alive in Orton the sense of his roots, illustrating his famous comment about not wanting people to forget his origins—the gutter. The other was a defensive weapon against inanity.

Orton's participation in neighborly conversations is joined by his habit of eavesdropping on people on buses or on the street. One that particularly fascinated him was the exchange between an old man and a woman on a bus. The diary entry bears striking resemblance to a sketch by Pinter of a conversation between two women waiting for a bus. Even the ominous note is there:

"What a thing, though," the old woman said. "You'd ardly credit it." "She's always made a fuss of the whole family, but never me," the old man said. "Does she have a fire when the young people go to see her?" "Fire?" "She won't get people seeing her without warmth." "I know why she's doing it. Don't think I don't," the old man said. "My sister, she said to me, 'I wish I had your easy life.' I was upset by the way she phrased herself. 'Don't talk to me like that,' I said. 'I've only got to get on the phone and ring a certain number,' I said, 'to have you stopped.' 'Yes,' the old woman said, 'and you can, can't you?'" "Were they always the same?" she said. "When you was a child? Can you throw yourself back? How was they years ago?" "The same," the old man said. "Wicked, isn't it?" the old woman said. "Take care now," she said, as the old man left her. He didn't say a word but got off the bus looking disgruntled. (*Diaries*, 68)

Pinter's sketch, "Request Stop," is an interior monologue of a woman in a queue for a bus as she attempts to engage a man in a conversation. Receiving no reply to her question about a bus to Shepherd's Bush, she takes umbrage with his silence, accusing him of insinuations and intentions of various sorts, one of these developing into a threat: "All I've got to do is to report you, and you'd be standing in the dock in next to no time. One of my best friends is a plain clothes detective."[3] Soon she is alone in line, even as another man comes along and she asks, "shyly, hesitantly, with a slight smile, 'Excuse me. Do you know if I can get a bus from here . . . to Marble Arch?'" (Pinter, 99).

Pinter's ear for naturalistic speech rhythms is deployed to dramatize dislocating inner psychological conflicts, whereas Orton's keen absorption of the bus conversation is one more illustration of his theory of language as a weapon—a word or phrase, according to Gombold in *Head to Toe*, that can unsettle or destroy: "Words were more effective than actions: in the right hands verbs and nouns could create panic. . . . The blast of a long sentence was curiously local, and a lot of shorter sentences seemed better."[4]

In his plays Orton uses the middle-class idiom as a lethal and hilarious weapon to destroy itself. The different uses to which the two writers

put the same kind of language support Orton's rejection of his writing as
Pinteresque, despite his admiration for Pinter and despite the
Pinteresque qualities of *The Ruffian on the Stair*.

One oft-referred-to real-life trick—another example of the writer's
detachment that Orton by then had perfected—is his presenting a
shocked cast of *Loot* with his mother's teeth, thinking they would like
"the originals." To the actor Kenneth Cranham, looking very sick and
shaking "like a jelly," Orton says, "You see, it's obvious that you're not
thinking of the events of the play in terms of reality, if a thing affects you
like that" (*Diaries*, 47). Also illustrating his insistence on reality is
Orton's description to Peggy Ramsay of his decrepit father, who "fumbling out of bed in the middle of the night bumped into the coffin and
almost had the corpse on the floor. Peggy said how dreadfully reminiscent of *Loot* it all was" (*Diaries*, 42).

Another motif throughout the *Diaries* is Orton's sexual life. With no
disguise of conventional morality with which to justify unconventional
acts, as in the plays, he narrates his sexual enounters with the same honesty and aplomb he displays in describing his mother's funeral, his visit
with the Beatles, or a weekend at the Brighton home of producer Oscar
Lewenstein. The earliest incident in the *Diaries* takes place after a visit to
Peggy Ramsay, with a copy of "An Unsavoury Interlude" (a two-minute
version of *The Ruffian on the Stair*), "which didn't come to anything"
(*Diaries*, 38). Orton meets an ugly Scotsman who "said he liked being
f———ed. He took me somewhere in his car and. . . . The sleeve of my
rainmac is covered in whitewash from the wall. It won't come off"
(*Diaries*, 38). Orton's linguistic ploy of ending a shocking action with a
familiar concern such as the whitewash is one that he so successfully uses
in his plays. In his diary entry it is as natural a reflex in his personal life
as is the socially unnatural act in which he has just engaged.

On his way to his family home for his mother's funeral, he "had a bit
of quick sex in a derelict house with a laborer I picked up" (*Diaries*, 42).
After the funeral he picked up a baggy Irishman who occupied a grimy
ground-floor room rented for sexual purposes. The encounter ended in
an equal exchange of sexual satisfaction. The two "talked for a while,"
and Orton was shown pictures of the man's fiancée. He concludes with a
comment about his amazement at the heavy molding of the ceiling, "a
centerpiece of acorns and birds painted blue" (*Diaries*, 43).

What is probably the most bizarre and humorous of Orton's flaunt-
ingly honest depictions is a multiple sexual fumbling in a men's lavatory
on the Holloway Road, eventually involving eight men. Following a dis-

astrous trip by Orton and Halliwell to Libya, the experience is one Orton recounted to Halliwell who said "It sounds as though eight pence and a bus down the Holloway Road was more interesting than £200 and a plane to Tripoli" (*Diaries*, 106). Nowhere in Orton's writing is the sexual sharing so seriously and hilariously presented.

Although the sexual episodes in or near men's lavatories in England are only a small part of the diary and exist in isolation from other events, those in Tangier are woven in with the routines of daily life. Both kinds of episodes—those in which Orton dangerously skirts the English legal system and those in Tangier in which the law is not even a consideration—honestly express Orton's exercising of freedom and his revenge on society's humiliation of that freedom. Disguises to the diarist are unnecessary, unlike those that prevail in his plays. Furthermore, unlike the Edna Welthorpes of his theater audiences, Orton defines pornography as hypocrisy and dishonesty, so that after watching an American film (*The Outlaw*) he describes it as "pornography with the pornography left out" (*Diaries*, 92). Orton's definition of pornography includes the gratuitous violence in American films and novels; he hoped that "the violence in my plays is not of an inconsequential nature" (Lahr 1978, 172).

Double Binds

On occasion Orton spoke of life's double binds—tricks played on him by society. In its most general sense the double bind in his experiences takes the form of destructive authoritarianism, which he described as "the old whore, society, [who] had lifted up her skirts" to emit a "foul stench" (*Diaries*, 28). Eventually Orton exorcised this double bind in his plays. Malodorous hypocrisy, especially that involving sexual attitudes, was a prime motivator of Orton's ingenious transmutation of low-life vulgarities into a farcical art distinct from that of any other dramatist.

In its most specific form, perhaps, he felt the double bind of the law during his six-month prison term—in his view unjust even as it developed in him the writer's necessary detachment. He exorcised this demon in such characters as Truscott, the unquestioned representative of justice who would take on whatever masks his position afforded to execute the mandate of injustice. He is both law enforcer and criminal.

Orton handled these double binds successfully. One that he could not control, however, was his relationship with Halliwell. At the time of their deaths Orton and Halliwell had for some time been involved with other sexual partners while maintaining their domestic arrangement. Grimmest of life's tricks was Orton's inability or unwillingness to see what his and Halliwell's acquaintances saw only too clearly—the dangerous psychopathy of Halliwell. As necessary educational and financial provider in the early days, he found himself becoming Orton's secretary and being left out of Orton's social life. No longer necessary, he could only watch as Orton's progress put into sharp focus his own lack of talent in both writing and collage painting. He is likened by Lahr to Vivien Eliot and Emma Hardy in their failure to deal with their husbands' successes.

The accumulation of Halliwell's real and imagined wounds burst out in a physical attack in Tangier, the result of Orton's taunting Halliwell about his masturbation habits as not virile. Orton's diary entry describing the episode (222), about six weeks before the murder-suicide, is one that Halliwell probably had read. Having had access to the diary with its progressive emphasis on Orton's growing pique at Halliwell's behavior, Halliwell grew more desperate. That desperation seemed not to propel Orton to immediate action. Ironically, the murder-suicide happened on the day that both had appointments that in themselves reflected Orton's success and Halliwell's failure. Orton was to see a producer about the filming of *Up Against It*, and Halliwell had an appointment with a new psychiatrist. In a neatly written note found on Orton's diary, Halliwell wrote,

> If you read his diary all will be explained. K.H.
> P.S. Especially the last part. (Lahr 1978, 3)

It was in that last part of the *Diaries* that Orton's frustration with their living arrangement was most intense. Halliwell's physical attack in Tangier in June of 1967 was then lethally repeated on 9 August 1967. In the end Orton was powerless to control a personal double bind at a time when his hard-won professional success had provided him with control, at least on stage, of that old whore, society.

With similarly grotesque irony, the epigraph to *The Ruffian on the Stair* from Henley's poem takes on significance. Death, the ruffian on the stair, had dogged Orton's life. Madame Life, the tenant of the room, blooms only during her short tenancy. As in Orton's plays, death runs like a motif in the *Diaries*, which begin and conclude with somber entries. Six days into the published diary entries (16 December 1966) Orton records the telephone call about his mother's death. The last entry (1 August 1967) is Orton's farewell to Halliwell, in connection with a visit to Leicester to attend a production of *Entertaining Mr. Sloane*. It reads, "Said goodbye to Kenneth this morning. He seemed odd. On the spur of the moment I asked him if he wanted to come home to Leicester with me. He looked surprised and said, 'No'" (*Diaries*, 265).

The horror of the final trick played on Orton, not by the law or any other representative of authority, but by death, puts into violent contrast the joyful and life-affirming clown-trickster who in his personal life skirted sexual laws and in his writing successfully raged against societal hypocrisy. A startling and occasionally uproarious self-portrait, the *Diaries* are both a literary triumph and Orton's final trick on life—his revenge on life-defeating forces in society. They are the final breaking of the double bind of which Orton spoke.

Critical Opinions

Orton's opinions on other writers and literature run through his *Diaries*. Although Orton is not here playing the trickster, he considers the ideas and theories of others with the same irreverence that had motivated his clownish jokes. They bear witness to the consistency of his independence, wit, and honesty. Some of his comments—for instance, what he writes about Enid Bagnold and Tennessee Williams—are gossip rather than literary criticism. Still, this is part of the unique texture of the *Diaries*, as much as Orton's low-life meanderings have been transmuted into art in his plays.

Seventeenth-century writers have a special affinity for Orton. As late as March 1967 Orton was reading *Gulliver's Travels* and setting down opinions on the major works of Jonathan Swift. Describing the Lilliput and Brobdingnag portions as "trick photography" and Laputa as "a bit strained," he favored the tale of the Yahoos as "the most superior part of the book" (*Diaries*, 126). The Yahoos may have confirmed Orton's views of contemporary society, particularly the characters of *What the Butler Saw*, which he was working on at the time. He much preferred *The Tale of a Tub* to *Gulliver's Travels*, and, agreeing with Samuel Johnson's assessment of Swift as an overrated writer, he thought fascination with Swift was due, "as with Dylan Thomas, Brendan Behan and many other writers," to their lives (*Diaries*, 126). With his personal life revealed in the *Diaries* and especially with the manner of his death, Orton, ironically, holds posthumous membership in this category of writers.

Orton's insistence on the naturalism of his characters is reflected in his judgment of William Congreve's *Love for Love*, whose style is one to be envied—"brilliantly written, perfectly believable. Nothing at all incredible" (*Diaries*, 141). Then after reading Richard Brinsley Sheridan's eighteenth-century farces, *The Rivals* and *The School for Scandal*, he pronounced them as "perfect plays" that are "worth any number of Restoration rubbish" (*Diaries*, 140). Unsuccessful in his search for collected volumes of plays by William Wycherley and George Farquhar, he settled for Thomas Middleton's *The Changeling*, upon advice from producer Peter Gill that he could use one of Middleton's subplots in his own play some day (*Diaries*, 144). It is the revenge plays of the seventeenth century, with their blood and social anarchy, that are closest to Orton's concerns. His use of an epigraph from Tourneur's *Revenger's Tragedy* in his last play only adds to that play's humorous violence, making it and Orton's other work closer to the traditions of Middleton and Tourneur than to the comedies of manners of Congreve and Sheridan, much as he admired the stylistic perfection of the latter two.

Orton's comments on novelists reflect his unsuccessful attempts at novel writing and a preference for the play genre because it can "obey the rules of a 'two hour traffic'" more easily than can the novel. On the same day that he gave up on Dostoyevski's *The Idiot* he found Virginia Woolf's *To the Lighthouse* wearying "with so much thought," yet admired it for its "beautiful prose stretching into infinity" (*Diaries*, 140).

With contemporary theater, Orton pays special attention to two famous dramatists who encouraged him early in his career—Pinter and Rattigan. Pinter was "the only contemporary English playwright besides himself that Orton admired" (*Diaries*, 35). The admiration was reciprocated by Pinter, who had gone so far as to liken the television production of *The Erpingham Camp* to the battleship *Potemkin* (*Diaries*, 78), an unusually extravagant comment for the normally restrained playwright. Despite their mutual admiration, Orton fiercely maintained his artistic independence. With confidence born of success, he eventually reversed the critics' comparisons with Pinter that had dogged reviews of *The Ruffian on the Stair*. Not only is this reversal obvious in succeeding plays, but also in his assertion that "*The Homecoming* [1965] couldn't have been written without *Entertaining Mr. Sloane* [1964]" (*Diaries*, 238). Pinter's debt, Orton claims, consists of the sexual sharing agreed to by Ruth in *The Homecoming*. Furthermore, although Orton admired the second act of *The Homecoming*, he did not think it was "true," since "Harold, I'm sure would never share anyone sexually. I would. And so *Sloane* springs from the way I think." The sexual sharing in Pinter's play "doesn't spring from the way Harold thinks" (*Diaries*, 238). Orton valued his professional association with Pinter, as seen in the many references to him in the *Diaries*, with the two playwrights sharing a number of the same directors and producers.

Orton's only literary criticism of Rattigan is his regret that he was unable to return Rattigan's critical praise "with any degree of conviction." Receiving his first fan letter from Rattigan, Orton responded, "I'd like to think I'd be as nice to somebody if I admired their writing" (*Diaries*, 114). As a master of plot construction himself, Rattigan called attention to the classical roots of Orton's plays. He went so far as to make suggestions about the relocation of a scene in *Entertaining Mr. Sloane*, advice from "an old hack," adding that the play would have had an additional three-months' run with the change. His comments included comparisons of Orton's style with that of Restoration comedies and of Wilde. He added that "in some ways it was better than Wilde because it had more bite. I was delighted by Orton's feeling for words" (Lahr 1978, 168, 169)—naturalistic, yet way beyond a naturalistic tradition.

Orton's acquaintance with Rattigan was personal as well as professional. He enjoyed a meal with Rattigan at London's fashionable Ivy Restaurant and a weekend at Rattigan's Brighton residence, in addition to financial support in the transfer of *Loot* to a larger theater. Rattigan called attention to Orton's unique dialogue as that of "a society diminished by telly-technology. Everybody expresses themselves as if they were brought up on television" (Lahr 1978, 153). Ronald Bryden's characterization of Orton's voice as that of welfare-state gentility, John Mortimer's label of Orton's stage speech as South Ruislip Mandarin, and Irving Wardle's description of it as as lower-middle-class Compton-Burnettese are reinforcements of Rattigan's general identification of the nature of Orton's distinctive stage language. Unlike the mutual stylistic admiration between Orton and Pinter, that with Rattigan was a one-way street, from Rattigan to Orton.

Another contemporary about whose first major play Orton reserved comment is Tom Stoppard. When *Rosencrantz and Guildenstern Are Dead* premiered at the Edinburgh Festival in 1966, two major plays by Orton and Pinter—*Loot* and *The Homecoming*—ran in London. Orton's judgment of Stoppard's play is one that has stood the test of time. Acknowledging its undergraduate and juvenile elements, he praised the "powerful and brilliant writing in it—particularly the scenes with the Player" (*Diaries*, 138). These are scenes with sexual references like those in Orton's own plays. In his expansive entry on the play, Orton sees derivations from Osborne's *Look Back in Anger* (1956) and *Waiting for Godot* (1953), both about "two bored people waiting for something to

happen and playing games to wile away the time" (*Diaries*, 134).
Wishing that he himself had stumbled on the wonderful idea of the play,
Orton notes that, unfortunately, the only drama in Stoppard's play is by
Shakespeare. The play "should've been about the futility of students—
always talking, talking, talking and never doing anything. Great events,
murders, adulteries, dreadful revenge happening all around them and
they just talk. This is what the play should've been about and wasn't"
(*Diaries*, 134).

Defiantly different from homosexual dramatists such as Wilde,
Coward, and Rattigan, Orton dared—in the 1960s, a time of worldwide
social upheavals yet one during which homosexuality dared not speak its
name—to speak a forbidden language. Writing his plays about unsuccessful male-female relationships in a more tranquil time just after
World War II, Rattigan had found it necessary to disguise all sexual matters in heterosexual terms. Orton, with his origins as he proudly proclaimed them, had nothing to lose and broke through barriers, much in
the way Osborne had done 10 years earlier—breaking an emotional
impasse on the English stage with his vitriolically emotional Jimmy
Porter in a culture that had sanctified the repressive, stiff-upper-lip, and
fair-play tradition for so long.

The *Diaries* confirm what his plays had already publicly expressed:
Orton as a force of nature. Like Gombold in *Head to Toe* who had prayed
for the ability to rage correctly, his rage was exposed rather than hidden
in the mask of laughter. Like Halliwell's suicide note saying that the
Diaries would explain the reason for the violent ends of the two men,
the *Diaries* serve to cast light on what the plays had already established:
Orton as the ultimate trickster of the age. Reading like a Swiftian novel,
they may be, in addition, Orton's revenge on his lack of success as a
novelist.

Chapter Three
Head to Toe and *Up Against It*

Orton's two nonstage works—a novel written before his successes in the theater (*Head to Toe*) and a screenplay (*Up Against It*) that was the reason for his intended visit to director Richard Lester on the day that Orton was murdered—serve as an interesting pair of bookends in Orton's career. Completed in 1961 and rejected by two publishers, *Head to Toe* is the novel Orton had hoped to rewrite some day. He was given that opportunity when Walter Shenson, producer of two Beatles' films—*A Hard Day's Night* and *Help!*—asked Orton to write a film for the Beatles. Orton looked forward to doing "all my box of tricks—Sloane and Hal on them. After all, if I repeat myself in this film it doesn't matter. No one who sees the film will have seen *Sloane* or *Loot*" (*Diaries*, 66).

The play eventually suffered the same fate as did the novel, when the script was returned without any accompanying explanation. It was then purchased by Oscar Lewenstein, and on 9 August 1967, when Orton was to meet with Richard Lester to discuss production of the film, Orton was bludgeoned to death by Halliwell. With the major characters of the script drawn from *Head to Toe*, Orton changed the nature of the novel by limiting the action to the romantic affair of his lead character and changing the mock-epic to a mock-romance that concludes with the three heroes happily marrying one woman—Orton's sexual sharing trick that he proudly talked about in regard to *Entertaining Mr. Sloane*.

The novel and script are symbiotically related in a number of ways. Both were rejected—the novel by two publishers in 1961 and the screenplay by the group who had commissioned it in the first place—and both are not in the genre that is the basis of Orton's fame.

Head to Toe: Seismic Disturbances

At the conclusion of *Head to Toe*, a giant, symbolic of the world whose hypocritical and destructive systems Orton attempted to disturb by creating panic with the use of verbs and nouns in the right hands, is dead.

Gombold, the hero of a picaresque novel in the tradition of Swift's Gulliver, had embarked on a strange journey in which he has strayed (like Dante) onto the head of a giant, hundreds of miles high. He falls into a hole, traveling down one side of the giant's body and then up the other. Innocently drawn into adventures such as the assassination of a prime minister and a war between the Left Buttocks and the Right Buttocks, he learns that that the pen is mightier than the sword and that panic—indeed, seismic disturbances—can be created with verbs and nouns in the right hands.

With an epic structure that is Dantean, a dream style that evokes Alice's adventures in Wonderland, and an autobiographical content that records the making of the artist, *Head to Toe* is the last of Orton's many novels—the earlier ones written jointly with Halliwell, this one singly. Completed in 1961 (published posthumously in 1971), the novel is a metaphor for Orton's life up to that time; in its broadest sense it is a mock-epic whose allusions to Dante, Virgil, Voltaire, and Rabelais seem haphazard at times yet are appropriate as part of the undisciplined nature of a dream. At one point Gombold and his friends take refuge in the Trojan Horse. At another, he meets Doktor von Pregnant, a Tiresias-like figure who looks about 2,000 years old and whose knowledge, much like Halliwell's in Orton's own life, is imparted to his student. Experimenting with the fanciful mixture of literary images and contemporary realities, Orton gives definition to ideas and techniques sharpened in the plays.

The novel clearly marks the end of Orton's unsuccessful writing of fiction, and in a life-imitating-art situation he, like Gombold, would shortly find himself serving a prison term. In a further irony, it was in prison that Orton, like his fictional hero, developed as a writer, frequently referring in later years to his acquiring an aesthetic detachment previously unrealized. In *Head to Toe* Orton defines the nature of that detachment he was later to realize. For Charles Monteith, an editor at the publishing house of Faber, the novel in 1961 was "several degrees too odd" and was turned down as a result. For Orton in 1967, when he reread the novel as a source for the Beatles film he was asked to write, the novel may have had its faults, "but as a basis for a film it was more than adequate" (*Diaries*, 76).

Readers may well question with Monteith the merits of the novel and agree with Lahr that *Head to Toe* was Orton's first crude attempt at using farce as an act of literary aggression (Gordon, 95). Authority, hypocrisy, anarchy, and the blurring of sexual identity are the important subjects for the peculiarly Ortonesque blending of humor and violence that Orton progressively perfected in his plays. In *Head to Toe* his aggressions are given full rein, and the novel becomes important in its deployment of the author's bag of tricks—tricks he has used in his plays and with which he has outraged audiences.

The novel is allegorically structured as a journey from head to toe and then toe to head of the giant on to whose head, some hundreds of miles high, Gombold, like Dante of the *Divine Comedy*, has strayed and found himself alone, frightened, and beset by a variety of dangers. The direction of the journey parodies the *Divine Comedy* as Gombold makes his way downward through his hell and then perversely upward toward his purgatory and paradise—the last resulting in his realizing how to "rage correctly." Gombold's travels include escapes from captors and prisons by way of swimming through sewers and into an ocean—again, a parody of the underground rivers of the Dantean universe. Gombold's physical journey ends, however, not in paradise but in the execution of his friends—Pill, O'Scullion, and Squall—after a trial conducted by Vulp and prosecuted by the fat man—the first humans he has encountered on his journey. Shortly thereafter Gombold discovers the death of the giant, and, depressed about the prospect of living on a corpse, he enters the wood for the last time and climbs down into a hole, the same hole involved in his initial experience in the novel.

In one of Gombold's earliest experiences, he is drawn into a revolution in which he kills, ironically, a woman prime minister. From that point on he finds himself in military struggles that culminate in the war between the Left Buttocks and Right Buttocks, one side eventually indistinguishable from the other. He undergoes a series of imprisonments much like those of Candide, Cunegonde, and Pangloss in Voltaire's *Candide*. Friends of Candide may be hanged or drawn and quartered, but they reappear miraculously, and Candide keeps running into former acquaintances. So it is with Gombold. There is also the satiric savagery of Swift's *Gulliver's Travels*, as Gombold encounters hostilities from characters who seem to embody the varying characteristics of Swift's Lilliputians, Brobdingnabians, and Yahoos. There are also the exaggerated aspects of Rabelais's Gargantua: Gombold's huge appetite for learning; the long, itemized descriptions; and the stylistic exaggerations such as that of the ball at the country house of Lord and Lady Beersheba, with their three million guests. If Candide's education consisted of the opposing theories of optimism and pessimism and Gargantua's the Renaissance world's desire for knowledge, Gombold's partakes of both the former's pessimism about the world and the latter's sating of intellectual appetite by means of instruction from Doktor von Pregnant, whose phenomenal memory enables him to recall in Joycean style the whole of "Shoxbear, Arrispittle, Grubben, Taciturn, Saint Trim-Dinty . . . and Kneetchur" (*Head*, 76).

But it is Dante whose influence is most in evidence from the start. Gombold, like Dante, has lost his way and finds himself in a wood, which turns out to be the hair of the giant. He encounters two combatants, and for helping them he is rewarded by one with a beating (the fattest man on earth) and by the other (Vulp, a mock-Virgil to Dante's guide) with desertion. In a later episode in which he meets Vulp again, Gombold accuses him of betraying his promise "to guide me through the wood" (*Head*, 17)—again an evocation of Dante's work.

Alone once more, Gombold is frightened by three animals—an eagle, a cock, and a lion—a parody of the leopard, lion, and she-wolf Dante meets in his famous journey. Throughout there are references to a woman, supposedly Gombold's mistress, named Beatrice, again a Dantean figure. Dante's three guides—Virgil, Beatrice, and Bernard—take various parodic forms in Gombold's experience. Through much of his journey, Gombold is accompanied by Pill and O'Scullion, whose main purpose, like Gombold's, is to survive—no reasoning Virgil, loving Beatrice, or spiritual Bernard these. Dante also makes it into *Entertaining Mr. Sloane*, wherein Orton's mock-epigrammatic style parodies Dante's epigraph to the *Divine Comedy* in Eddie's accusation of his sister Kath: "You showed him the gate of hell every night. He abandoned hope when he entered there."[1]

Having met humans and animals, with the attendant dire consequences, Gombold adds to Dante's animals and humans a curious third group of creatures from the plant world—truffles, pumpkins, carrots, daisies, melons, loganberries, weeds, leaves, thistles, and the rose, William Orton's favorite flower—who war with each other no less than do their counterparts in the animal world. Having already asked directions from the animals and experiencing only fear and rebuffs, Gombold hesitates to make the same requests of plant lives. One floral voice illustrates Orton's freshly turned clichés: "I wouldn't be closeted with a carrot for all the tea in China." Claude, a loganberry, gloating over having scratched a picker whose fingers were "five hideous things plunging down," complains that "It's enough to turn a raspberry pale" (*Head*, 13). Orton's delightful wonderland will soon become a violent universe, but for this brief moment in the novel his talking plants even discuss various plant books—*Simple Vegetable Arrangement, Vegetables for Decoration*, and *Plants of the Bible*—all recalling the many gardening books Orton and Halliwell had borrowed from a public library and defaced.

Whereas Orton's father's lifelong interest in plants is recognizable as a source for the flowers episode, his mother, Elsie, influenced the novel in a less direct way. With a change in names the following passage could easily have been a part of the dialogue in *Entertaining Mr. Sloane*. The imprisoned Gombold and Squall spend their time exchanging stories, one of which involves a dwarf, who suggests the diminutive size and nature of Orton's father, dominated by his extroverted wife:

"That dwarf I was telling you about," he said one day.
  "Are you interested?"
  "Yes," Gombold said.
  "I thought you might be."
  "What was his wife like?"
  "She was a bit of a mystery. Her name was Emmy. She used to work for a firm of wholesale chemists before her marriage."
  "My mother's name was Emmy."
  "It's a name you feel confident with. My own Ma's maiden name was Annie. Annie Francine Bridie Trull. She died many years ago now. She passed away three weeks after my sister was married." (*Head*, 69)

In a Pinter-like deflection of emphasis, Gombold asks, "Is she happily married?" Squall responds with another shift: "She is getting a place of her own soon." The subsequent conversation is the kind in which a Nurse Fay engages in *Loot*:

"Has she any children?"
  Squall drew in his breath. "She's not likely to be breeding," he said. "She married Christ. She had a vocation." (*Head*, 69)

Squall ends his story with a reference to his mother's being embalmed and her wish "to be scientifically preserved." Orton's ear for conversational idiom and his ironic wit in distorting conventional patterns of thinking and speaking permeates the novel. These patterns are there not only in his plays but in the many conversations in his *Diaries*. The macabre detail of embalming and scientific preservation is like that regarding the coffin and casket that contain the remains of Mrs.

McLeavy in *Loot*. Death and funeral rites are prominent in Orton's plays and are integral to his comic aggression against the giantism of authoritarian forces in his life.

Gombold recurringly confronts holes in the giant's body, each hole propelling him into a new adventure and emphasizing the topsy-turvy nature of the world—much as the rabbit hole did for Alice. Near one hole, Gombold is beaten for his attempts to help a fat man who turns into the prosecutor at the trial of Gombold's three friends at the end. Alice's tea party is rendered as the hospitality that is offered at some times but denied at others. There is, as in Alice's land, the continual aura of the dream world. Gombold dreams frequently, with one of his more disturbing nightmares involving a "goat, father of Fornicationists, preaching chastity, a big-bellied virgin, a pair of pink combinations. . . . He saw twelve figures armed with sickles hacking away his testicles," his castration "the seed of God" giving "form to the formless" (*Head*, 82). Orton ends this nightmare with the kind of line that became a stylistic hallmark in his plays—the undercutting of nightmarish violence with a return to daylight reality. Gombold wakes from his dream crying and "continued to moan to himself until the warder entered with breakfast" (*Head*, 82). Gombold's prison experience also has its moments of isolation, eerily foreshadowing Orton's, in which the only "communicants were men of his imagination . . . who peopled the silence and told him of their lives" (*Head*, 70).

Orton's seriously farcical concerns are expressed in his curious combination of authority and anarchic sexual identities in an early incident in which Vulp appears. Enraged by Gombold's break-in and interruption of a bedroom episode, Vulp and his wife call for help. A fat policewoman appears, and, embracing Gombold, provides him with his first bit of comfort. Her sexualized humanity is as natural as his assumption of his role as her wife. Orton's blurring of sexual identity—a recurring theme that involves transvestism—is the essence of the plot of his last stage play, *What the Butler Saw*. Gombold even promises never to wear "Daddy's clothes," for a time contentedly wearing a frilly apron. But he is soon tempted by the idea of the power in the male clothes that she wears and elatedly dons them as he begins a new series of adventures.

Among Gombold's many adventures, one of the most curious is his meeting in prison with a Doktor von Pregnant, a rebel like himself who, although his side had won, had been thrown into prison. The doctor has concocted elaborate plans for escape and has written his life's work, *A Concise History of the World and Its Interests*, on paper he has made from several shirts. Like Rabelais's Gargantua, Gombold is tutored by the doctor, patterned after Halliwell, who broadened Orton's literary horizons. Gombold wonders "if the Doktor were not one of his waking visions" (*Head*, 76). In a parody of Ben Jonson's tribute to Shakespeare's learning, Gombold confesses to "little Litthom and less Glook" (*Head*, 77). The two sketch out a plan of education that includes "Glook, Litthom and Hoobray, Trukkish and the many dialect forms of Greeman" (*Head*, 79). They also discuss Sir Thomas Browne, Petrarch and Laura, and Achilles. As the doctor talks, Gombold dreams. The doctor is the intellectual and Gombold the artist. When they finally escape, having swum sewers and ocean and landed on a shore, the old doctor peacefully dies. His death contrasts ironically with the violent suicide of Halliwell.

Having completed his education, Gombold "had broken from his chrysalis and emerged whole" (*Head*, 86). With the sense of detachment Orton said he developed during his prison time, his education by Halliwell was also completed, and Gombold's wholeness was Orton's, one that the fictional hero expressed in a Joycean elation of being "part and parcel of the world, of the ocean, of the universe," yet conscious of the water and the "great waves determined to dash him to pieces on the rocks, to smash his freedom before he had tasted it" (*Head*, 86). In the grip of an eagle, he was flown over the giant's body, and they fell "towards the city situated between the navel and the groin" (*Head*, 88). Gombold's dreamlike experience recalls that of Joyce's Stephen Dedalus and the maiden along the shore calling him to his vocation.

Not until the end of a series of harrowing experiences in a constantly changing and chaotic political scene does the subject of Gombold's writing come up. He realizes that "words are more effective than actions; in the right hands verbs and nouns could create panic" (*Head*, 174). He is motivated by his repugnance to a popular dramatist, Offjenkin, who "had made an attempt to design a sentence which would speak for itself, but had abandoned the idea as too destructive" (*Head*, 174). Gombold then bought a dictionary in order to study the construction of a sentence, and he "studied the behaviour of words, phrase design, the forging, casting and milling, the theories of paraphrase and periphrase, the fusing and the aiming" (*Head*, 175). His study included "the propagation of idiom . . . and came up with a preliminary theoretical answer. A sentence no more than six words long, with no adjectives and in the second person plural, should result in the complete collapse of the enemy power" (*Head*, 175). Lahr records in his biography that Orton had made a practice of compiling long lists of words, probably like those described by Gombold.

Gombold then sets out to get people to listen to his theories, and he tries out his theories on people he meets in the city, finding some sentence failures. Upon questioning a boy whose sentence had caused an old woman to react immediately, he realizes that the sentence used by the boy "was quite simple in construction." In the end, with his friends and the giant dead and the popular dramatist accusing Gombold of being one of them, Gombold, noticing the mile upon mile of putrescent countryside, burns Vulp's house and climbs down into the hole.

In 1964, three years after the completion of *Head to Toe* (originally titled *The Vision of Gombold Proval*), Orton's first play, *The Ruffian on the Stair*, was broadcast on BBC Third Programme, and with his first success Orton realized the truth of Gombold's words—that "to be destructive words had to be irrefutable," and that spoken rather than printed words, if one could "lock the enemy into a room somewhere," would "create some sort of seismic disturbance" (*Head*, 175). The productions of his plays, beginning with *Entertaining Mr. Sloane*, produced the intended seismic waves from some management impresarios and from the Edna Welthorpes of the theater world, but the play also brought accolades from such peers as Terence Rattigan and Harold Pinter. Had Orton lived to see the publication of the novel in 1971, he would have read Auberon Waugh's proclamation of it as "worthy of Swift."

Up Against It: Anarchy in Full Bloom

Having aimed his farcical gun at the law in *Entertaining Mr. Sloane*, the institution of the holiday camp in *The Erpingham Camp*, corporate impersonality in *The Good and Faithful Servant*, religion in *Funeral Games*, and psychiatry in *What the Butler Saw*, Orton decided to make the romance tradition another target. Having parodied the comedy of manners, the detective genre, and the farce, he turned to the romantic traditions of love and war. Love as sex and ideology as chaos are Orton's means of smashing conventional attitudes.

Derived from *Head to Toe*, *Up Against It* is the kind of pure farce Orton had just completed in *What the Butler Saw*. Extracting the action and some characters from the novel, he changes the introspective Gombold into a romantic McTurk, whose actions are determined by his love for Rowena. Gombold, a realized character of the novel, is replaced by

McTurk, a caricatured Don Juan and Orton's spokesman for the destruction of romantic myths even as he uses those very myths to accomplish his purpose.

In 129 fast-moving scenes, the farce is tailored to the style of the action movie. Written in 1967, when President Kennedy's 1963 assassination was still on the minds of the public, the timing of the script may have had something to do with its rejection by the Beatles. Ironically, two more political assassinations—of Robert Kennedy and Martin Luther King in 1968—were to come, as was the attempted assassination of Britain's first woman prime minister, Margaret Thatcher, in 1984.

Love, politics, revolution, and financial greed fuel the plot, beginning with the exiling of McTurk and Low by Father Brodie and the Mayor (Terence O'Scallion) and concluding with the marriage ceremony performed by Brodie in the presence of O'Scallion. Forced into exile by his undying love for Rowena, McTurk sets off with Low on a series of adventures resembling those of Gombold in *Head to Toe*. There is the same opening episode of the adventure with a fat man imprisoned in a hole and another who turns on Low even as Low comes to his aid.

McTurk and Low are joined eventually by Ramsay, whose father is dedicated only to the idea of revolution, regardless of its nature. All four participate in revolution and counterrevolution, to the point that no one seems to know who is on which side and what the fighting is about. Ramsay enlists them for his current project, the assassination of the prime minister, Lillian Corbett. At a political convention in Royal Albert Hall, he tells them of his aim to "undermine people's confidence in the government of the day."[2] To do so he advocates the tactics of "the smear, the lie, and, in extreme cases, even the truth." In McTurk and Low, Orton has fun re-creating the nature of Hal in *Loot* and of Nick in *What the Butler Saw*—men whose compulsive truth-telling, in their otherwise nefarious actions, only creates new difficulties for all. McTurk and Low thus accommodate with ease Ramsay's instruction to tell the truth.

Up Against It is an uninhibited parody of the romance genre. Set in the context of a bloody political uprising, Orton's devastatingly funny attack is his final tribute to the id-releasing sexual anarchy that, by 1967, had become his recognized metaphor for the demolition of authoritarianism. Romance is wickedly lampooned, most obviously in scenes such as the balcony scene of *Romeo and Juliet*. McTurk, unlike the renegade writer that is Gombold in *Head to Toe*, is Romeo to Rowena's Juliet. He loves her forever, even though she and others constantly refer to her as the most modern woman in the world. As such, she rejects him in favor of the rich Coates, the screenplay's version of Vulp. Because he is rich, Coates can afford to have bad teeth and to possess Rowena as his wife. Rowena and McTurk clandestinely meet from time to time in settings loaded with romantic clichés—moonlight, roses, nightingale, and waltz—which are continuously undercut by realities such as a bloody war, prison for McTurk, and a very modern version of Juliet. In Orton's parodic heaven, Rowena responds impatiently to McTurk's assertion that she has been constantly in his thoughts throughout his sufferings: "I must go. Love seems out of place in a garden in the moonlight" (*Against*, 64). Though McTurk endures blow after blow, he is rewarded with the requisite happy ending, but one that is distinctively Ortonesque. He and two companions, Low and Ramsay, marry not Rowena but Patricia Drumgoole, who in earlier appearances panders to Rowena and McTurk—a parody of Juliet's nurse in Shakespeare's play.

Exile is the lot of the romantic McTurk, like Gombold's in *Head to Toe*, and so he and Low are led, early in the play, to the outskirts of the city, accompanied by the ritual procession headed by Father Brodie, the Mayor, and an assortment of civic dignitaries. McTurk's crime was sex with Rowena who was seen entering his room nude, and Low's was the blowing up of the War Memorial, an allegorical statue of the figure of Peace. His remonstrance that he was only placing a wreath at the monument at the request of a World War II veteran met with no success. Orton had already used the consequences of the blowing of a national monument (Winston Churchill's statue) in *What the Butler Saw* as one of several climaxes in that play.

At a low ebb in McTurk's fortunes, he escapes from a yacht and, washed ashore, awakes to find himself taken care of by none other than Connie, the policewoman who coincidentally appears whenever nourishment or comfort is necessary, with her price being only sexual favors. The incident, like the Haidee episode in Byron's *Don Juan*, is one in which nature, uncomplicated by human institutions, is allowed to take its course. Far from the purity of Haidee, however, Connie is a rising politician who exerts her influence at will, especially in McTurk's favor whenever the opportunity presents itself.

During one of several prison terms, McTurk complains of the conditions, only to find himself moved to yet a worse cell. Like Gombold, he escapes by digging a hole into a sewer, swimming to the open sea. Washed ashore, he once more finds himself being aided and consoled by Connie, who enlists him on her side. Asked whom they are fighting, Connie replies, "The rebels, of course." She overlooks his confession of sympathy with the rebels and gives him an alcohol rub as a "sort of parting present."

Evoking yet another work in which romantic traditions are deflated, Voltaire's *Candide*, Orton has people who have been thought dead reappear constantly, among these Patricia Drumgoole, who reintroduces herself as the graduate of Father Brodie's pantry and is eventually the bride of the three adventurers. Candide's undying love for Cunegonde, however ugly she has become over the years, is matched by McTurk's for Rowena, however much the latter rejects him in favor of the ugly but rich Coates. Candide's philosopher-tutor, Pangloss, finds a double in the Ramsays, who are only shadows of the Panglossian Doktor von Pregnant in *Head to Toe*.

Wars between good and evil, at the heart of the medieval romantic tradition, take the form here of conflicting modern ideologies. They involve a series of revolutions in which the current matriarchy is constantly being threatened by the males. Both the prime minister and the archbishop of Canterbury are women, and the men fall into three groups: those drawn in for financial greed (Coates and O'Scallion), those who only want to survive (McTurk and Low), and those for whom anarchy is its own reason for being (the Ramsays, father and son).

In a bedraggled state, Ramsay's father at one point acknowledges the muddle he has made of the fighting. McTurk, still romantic, promises to have him "safe and sound in a well-run all-male hospital" (*Against*, 58). But the elder statesman, in another of his constant turnabouts in the name of anarchy, will have nothing to do with the promise. Instead he intends to join the rebels: "Back to the women! Our only hope!" (*Against*, 58).

In a climactic scene, the big battle is not strategically planned but, rather, accidentally begun by a crashing of an ambulance into a lorry, ending in such violence that even the stretcher bearers have to be fought off. No one seems to know who is the enemy, and thus everyone is one's potential enemy. The scene is another of Orton's "tricks," resembling the bloody crash in the funeral procession in *Loot* and the climactic piling up of bodies in all states of dress and mistaken identities in *What the Butler Saw*.

Orton's only original film script is as interesting for the ironic circumstances surrounding its unrealized production as for its literary merit. To date it has not been produced. In the midst of his most successful year, 1965—*Loot*'s success in the West End, the sale of *Loot* for a movie production, a revision of *The Erpingham Camp* for a new double-bill production with *The Ruffian on the Stair* as *Crimes of Passion*—Orton wrote the commissioned screenplay that was eventually rejected by the Beatles' management with no explanation. It was subsequently purchased by Oscar Lewenstein, a director for Woodfall Productions, among whose cinematic successes were *Tom Jones* and *A Taste of Honey*. Lewenstein thought Orton's to be the "best first draft of a screen-play I have ever read" (Lahr 1978, 251). Orton's last dramatic legacy to the world—although Lewenstein had writers Charles Wood, James Saunders, Roger McGough, and Christopher Logue work on the script—resisted all efforts to improve it, and it remains "a tantalizing remnant of what might have been, the last comic fragment of a voluptuary of fiasco" (*Against*, xvi).

Orton originally intended "four bridegrooms and one bride. *The Homecoming* [Pinter's play that had premiered in 1965] in fact, but alibied in such a way that no one could object. Lots of opportunities for sexual ambiguities" (*Diaries*, 64). In Pinter's play Ruth deserts her husband, a professor of philosophy in America, in order to remain with her husband's father and two brothers who will set her up as a prostitute. *Up Against It* ends with the carrying of the bride over the threshold by her three bridegrooms—Orton's farcical perfecting of Eddie and Kath's sharing of Sloane in *Entertaining Mr. Sloane*. Also, in his early stages of writing the script, Orton had thought of writing the four characters as one composite figure but then changed his mind, creating instead three separate characters.

Staged as a musical on 4 December 1989 at New York's Public Theater, it failed in the hands of, as Mel Gussow described them, misguided admirers who manage to "obliterate whatever charm existed in the screenplay."[3] The effort to create a stage musical from a film musical ran into all kinds of production difficulties as "book, score, direction, perfomances even the push-me, pull-you plasterboard scenery" (Gussow, 17), collided with disastrous results. In its unproduced cinematic form, *Up Against It* remains an ironic witness to Orton's unfinished career and life.

Chapter Four
Crimes of Passion

Four short plays—*The Ruffian on the Stair, The Erpingham Camp, The Good and Faithful Servant*, and *Funeral Games*—constitute Orton's quartet of originally nonstage dramatic writing. With the success of *Entertaining Mr. Sloane* and *Loot* having solidly established Orton's reputation as a new voice on the English stage by 1967, he decided to revise for the stage two short plays under the title *Crimes of Passion*. Originally aired on radio and television, respectively, *The Ruffian on the Stair* (31 August 1964) and *The Erpingham Camp* (27 June 1966) concentrate on passions—private in the earlier play, private and collective in the latter. In each of Orton's three major plays the actions rise to a moment in which passions gathering throughout the play end in violence, followed by a return to the situations that led to the crime in the first place. No legal or moral punishment is involved. This pattern is first present in *The Ruffian on the Stair*, in which the passion for revenge is private and deliberate, as demonstrated in the order given by the victim to his assassin: "The heart is situated just below the badge on my pullover. Don't miss, will you?" (*Plays*, 54). In *The Erpingham Camp* the passion is a collective one against authority, the chief representative of which issues his final instructions to the rebels just before his death: "I shall confiscate your luggage. What is your chalet number?" (*Plays*, 316).

The "crimes" of Orton's new title are usual in his plays, as seen in his declaration of all classes as criminal. The "passion" of the title refers to people's instinctive rebellion against societal misrule. "A holiday from the established order" (Lahr 1978, 17), Orton's plays are fiendish in their celebration of the brief moment when anarchy upsets order. It is doubtful that Mike in the earlier play and the revelers in the later play will be punished, but both private and collective rebels have realized the seismic disturbance at which Gombold in *Head to Toe* aimed and, more importantly, for which Orton's own disturbing of the clichéd order of everyday speech has crowned him, in Lahr's terms, the Lord of Misrule (Lahr 1978, 17).

The Ruffian on the Stair: "A Tale Told by a Commercial Traveller"

Orton's first short play was aired on radio, BBC's Third Programme, in 1964. Its history reflects the manner in which Orton wrote and rewrote. Derived from his (and Halliwell's) unpublished novel, *The Boy Hairdresser*, the radio version as published by the BBC in 1966 was prohibited by Orton for further publication. Orton rewrote the radio script for television and then again for the stage for "a performance without decor" at the Royal Court Theatre (1966), a version to become part of *Crimes of Passion* (1967). The title character of the novel and play identifies himself as a "Gent's Hairdresser." The epigram to the play, a stanza from a poem by W. E. Henley, contains the title of Orton's play:

> Madam Life's a piece in bloom
> Death goes dogging everywhere:
> She's the tenant in the room
> He's the ruffian on the stair. (*Plays*, 29)

A combination of mystery, murder, revenge, sex, and a preoccupation with death, the play is a mixture of ingredients to be found in many of Orton's plays. In five scenes the action moves rapidly, beginning, as does Pinter's *The Room*, with a breakfast conversation between Joyce and Mike, who live together in a small, dreary flat. Like Bert Hudd in *The Room*, Mike drives a van. He informs Joyce that he will not be using the van this day as it is in the shop for repairs. Like Bert's, the nature of Mike's work is uncertain and mysterious, but it involves appointments with shady characters. He informs Joyce that on this day he has an appointment with a contact in the men's toilet of the King's Cross Station. Joyce's response to what seems to the audience an unusual situation is in the form of routine, commonplace idiom that derails audience expectation: "You always go to such interesting places" (*Plays*, 31). This unsettling disjunction between play and audience is a stylistic hallmark for which Orton is famous. The autobiographical element, strong in Orton's early plays, draws on his familiarity with men's lavatories.

Joyce reminds Mike that it is the second anniversary of their meeting in which Mike persuaded her to give up her life as a prostitute to live with him. Her dull life in contrast with Mike's or in contrast with her former life is about to change, for after his departure an unexpected male stranger, Wilson, a "gent's hairdresser," makes an appearance to apply for a room vacancy that does not exist, disrupting the routine of what had promised to be just another day for Joyce. Wilson's further disquieting knowledge about Joyce's past and present life and even about the physical details of the apartment is Pinteresque in its menacing nature.

The scene seems right out of *The Room*, in which Riley suddenly appears after Bert has left for work. Riley, as with Orton's Wilson, inquires of Rose Hudd about a room, raising her fears about possible displacement from the flat. He also creates mystery by addressing Rose by names from her past, but unlike that of Wilson, his mystery remains even at the play's end.

Wilson returns the next day in what seems an attempted break-in. He smashes windows and loosens locks, yet he does not enter, adding more mystery and suspense to his appearance. A third intrusion, this time when Mike is at home, is different from the first two, since, although hostile at first, Mike decides, against Joyce's warning, to admit Wilson as a lodger, partly at least because of his and Wilson's common Irish heritage. In yet another surprising turnabout, Mike falls into a trap set by Wilson to avenge Mike's killing of Wilson's brother with his van. The mousetrap consists of Wilson's well-planned feigning of sexual advances on Joyce. With no will to live after his brother's death, Wilson wishes only to live long enough to avenge the death. He carries out his plot to provoke Mike into shooting him, thus ensuring Mike's eventual arrest. Wilson's revenge involves a motif that is woven throughout the play— the suggested incestual-homosexual relationship between Wilson and his brother that Wilson claims to be stronger than the heterosexual relationship between his brother and Joyce in earlier days. The relationships are clear; they do not present the enigmas of Pinter's play.

The play's images are reminiscent not only of *The Room* but also of Pinter's *The Dumb Waiter* and *The Birthday Party*. Orton's murder suggests the assassination in *The Dumb Waiter*, whose plot has been frequently compared with that of Hemingway's short story "The Killers," produced on screen in 1946. The film is one that both Pinter and Orton may have seen, in the light of Orton's comments that he and Pinter were influenced by the same movies of the 1940s. One of Pinter's two hired assassins—uneasy chums in the course of the play—turns out to be the murderer of the other. Just so, Mike, falling unwittingly into Wilson's scheme, becomes the murderer of his "guest."

Similarities to *The Birthday Party* include the mother-whore character, another recurrent Orton's motif. A variation of Meg Boles in Pinter's play, Joyce is older than the young intruder and, of course, than Wilson's brother with whom she had had an earlier sexual relationship. Also, just as Meg's young visitor, Stanley, is carried away by men in a van, Mike, after he murders Wilson, may be taken away by the police.

One important change Orton made to the stage version of *The Ruffian on the Stair* was the elimination of the opening breakfast conversation with its banalities about the "nice cornflakes"—a very clear borrowing from a similar "nice eggs" dialogue in the opening of *The Birthday Party*. His attempt to mute the chorus of Pinter comparisons that accompanied earlier versions of the play is evident in his shortening of the opening dialogue. Despite his attempts, the similarities persist.

In at least two major ways, however, Orton is most un-Pinteresque. He packs his tale of revenge with as much explanatory detail as a brief play can accommodate. Pinter's subtextual technique, on the other hand, is one of withholding as much detail as possible, especially the kind that clearly establishes relationships and motivations. His highly minimalist style is itself the means for creating mystery and suspense, whereas in Orton's work the physical actions do so.

In *not* withholding information Orton wishes the audience to have, he reveals that in her days as a prostitute Joyce has known Wilson's brother. Joyce's fears in the first scene—as she talks with Mike about a newspaper account of a van accident and Mike mentions that his van is still in the repair shop—are confirmed by Wilson. He increases her fears with his thoroughly researched knowledge of her living arrangements with Mike. He even knows where the gun is, though Joyce denies its existence. He slowly builds his case against Mike, using Joyce's past as part of his revenge plan. Revenge rather than menace and certainty rather than mystery are the elements of Orton's work. The unexpected intruder who arrives one day to apply for lodgings unfolds an intricately detailed story that involves all three characters in a web of circumstances as old as Greek tragedy, with the incestual detail and need for revenge bringing to mind Shakespeare's *Hamlet*.

The surprise of the play is Wilson's carefully drawn plot to avenge his brother's death. All is explained, including Wilson's revenge-suicidal obsession since the death of his brother. He plans to have Mike shoot him after catching him in a liaison with Joyce. Like Hamlet's mousetrap, Wilson's revenge is complete. This clarity of motivation and actions is foreign to Pinter's style, and herein is the major dfference between Orton and Pinter. It is the beginning of Orton's distinctive style that in succeeding plays progressively diminishes any subtleties of character motivations and replaces them with broad actions and witty dialogue that have earned for him the description "Ortonesque."

Pinter's sparse and carefully selected details are at the core of the never-ending psychological or sexual contests in which characters achieve or protect their security by gaining power over each other. To this end Pinter uses rooms, intrusions on those rooms, dislocations in which physical positions of sitting and standing are symbolic of power shifts, and minuscule actions such as the famous glass-of-water scene between Ruth and Lenny in *The Homecoming* to show contests for dominance.

In contrast, Orton insists that his plays be performed naturalistically, rather than with stylization or "camp" (Lahr 1978, 130)—a distinction between his plays and Pinter's that he has emphasized on a number of occasions. The naturalism is illustrated in Orton's outrageously offensive combination of low-life language—filthy to those who only hear it literally—and sophisticated satire. The wit, however plentiful in the play, is overshadowed by the melodramatic actions and revelations. Yet there are enough examples to provide a foretaste of what to expect in his best writing. There is, for example, the absurd mixture of biblical, Shakespearean, and contemporary images in Mike's outburst upon hearing Joyce's account of Wilson's actions. Orton's ear for the aphoristic language of the common man is unerring:

What's she up to? (*pause*) I'll maybe forgive her. Our Lord forgave the woman taken in adultery. But the circumstances were different. (*pause*) It's a ludicrous business. Ludicrous. The deceit. At her age. She wants somebody younger. At her age they get the itch. It's like a tale told by a commercial traveller. Just for a few minutes' thrill. I don't know what she'd be like if we had a television. (*Plays*, 56)

Mike and Wilson find bonds—their Irish Catholic backgrounds, their welfare status, and their views of women as bitches not to be trusted. Wilson offers his view that it is "the Latin temperament that has been the curse of our religion," and he desires to see "a Liffey man on the throne of St Peter." His speech has the lyricism of Sean O'Casey's: "I'd be proud to hear the Lateran ring with the full-throated blasphemies of our native land" (*Plays*, 47). To Mike's response that "the Vicar of Christ doesn't blaspheme," Wilson replies, "He would if he was Irish and drank Guinness" (*Plays*, 47).

In the type of unsettling wit that has become a hallmark of Orton's style, Mike, infuriated by Wilson's revelations of intimate details of Joyce's past, characterizes Wilson's story as "a tale told by a commercial traveller" (*Plays*, 56). This parody of *Macbeth* is an early example of Orton's epigrammatic style that is sometimes derived from classical sources, in addition to the clichés of everyday speech. Mike soliloquizes on Joyce's "being the biggest old tart since the mother of Solomon" (*Plays*, 55) and on the country's being full of whores and communists.

Orton's turns of wit are a natural expression of his experiences. Like Wilson, he feels trapped in a world that has deprived him of what he values most in life, as with his experiences with the National Assistance Board. Turning a cliché on its head, he has Wilson complain of the board's advice to alter his circumstances when, as he claims, there are no circumstances to alter. Wilson's economic entrapment is shared by Mike, who has only the odd criminal job and Joyce left.

Wilson's concern with death echoes Orton's throughout his published and unpublished work. Even the man Mike had met at the King's Cross toilet (another echo of Orton's life) is dogged by death, the ruffian on the stair. He had bad feet and "looked as though life had treated him rough" and "hadn't much to live for" (*Plays*, 37). Wilson and Mike, destined as enemies, even enjoy a short companionship to which Joyce is hostile. A similar companionship exists in the autobiographical characters of Peterson and Donnelly in Orton and Halliwell's *The Boy Hairdresser*, from which *The Ruffian on the Stair* is drawn.

Orton's alienation in his familial, sexual, and social life and his living on the dole for so many years are reflected in the circumstances of Wilson. When Orton wrote the play he was nearing the end of his first 10 years in London, which had at best left him unfulfilled and at worst offered only more failures to look forward to.

Unlike Jimmy Porter, John Osborne's university-educated and angry antihero of the first wave of the English stage revolution in the mid-1950s, Wilson, like Orton, is from the gutter and coldly calculates his actions. He is a different kind of hero for the second wave of the revolution: neither intellectual nor angry, he is hopeless and bent only on death. He is detached from life and suggests the many comments of Orton about the necessary detachment he acquired during his imprisonment. The detachment allows Wilson to be aggressive and to boast a bit about giving satisfaction to gents whose hair he had cut. Orton's own detachment enabled him increasingly to flaunt his life-style in his writings.

Wilson is the first of a number of autobiographical characters throughout Orton's plays. In *Entertaining Mr. Sloane* Wilson is reinvented in Sloane, the major difference being the latter's survival instincts. As a pair of Orton's innocents, Wilson and his dead brother are a variation of character pairs that recur in later plays: Sloane and Eddie in *Entertaining Mr. Sloane*, Hal and Dennis in *Loot*, the twins in *The Good and Faithful Servant*, and Geraldine and Nick in *What the Butler Saw*. In their representation of the varying facets of the long relationship between Orton and Halliwell, the pairs illustrate a naturalness or innocence that has been humiliated or destroyed by a guilt-inducing, authoritarian society.

Among the many motifs to be found in this, Orton's first play—revenge, detective-style mystery, the mother-whore character, homosexuality, incest—death is what links it to all Orton's other plays, except his last. The ruffian Death is absent, but the blood and violence remain—only they are transmuted into mocking laughter that stretches the limits of Congreve and Wilde in their comedy of manners and creates a modern farce-tragedy more akin to the seventeenth-century tradition of Cyril Tourneur's *Revenger's Tragedy*, so that comparisons of *What the Butler Saw* are more likely to be with Tourneur than with Pinter.

The Erpingham Camp

Written in 1965 and first produced on Rediffusion Television on 27 June 1966, *The Erpingham Camp* became the second part of *Crimes of Passion*, produced by the English Stage Company at the Royal Court Theatre in 1967. In this short, 11-scene farce Orton departs from the personalized or melodramatic style of *The Ruffian on the Stair* and other of his preceding plays—*Entertaining Mr. Sloane*, *The Good and Faithful Servant*, and even *Loot*, which contains a residue of human sympathy in the character of McLeavy. *The Erpingham Camp* is Orton's first totally detached farcical attack on authority. Within the highly organized holiday camp Orton constructs and deconstructs a collage of societal forces—religion, sexuality, domestic and foreign politics, and music, painting, and literature.

When given the opportunity, the camp's law-abiding citizens break ranks with authorities in an orgy of violence. As the ultimate authority, government and the Empire variety of English nationalism are allegorically vested in Erpingham, the leader of the camp. He even impersonates the queen, when, properly costumed, he grants an audience to the queen herself—that is, to a photograph of the queen.

With such an absolute and rigid leader, it is inevitable that the campers—even though they represent Orton's welfare-state gentility—rebel. In fact, they are no less the object of hilarious satire than are the camp authorities. Eventually anarchy replaces order, and the camp is once more an insane asylum run by the insane. Erpingham is abetted in his insanity by a representative of the Christian church, named merely Padre. When "the rabble, led by their leader, approaches the very door of Government," Erpingham readies himself and his cohorts for the onslaught with his pronouncement: "Clothed in the glory of God the Church approaches!" (*Plays*, 314). Padre responds to Erpingham's question about the management of the rebellion with one of the funniest verbal conceits of the play: "Have no worries, Chief Redcoat Riley. It's life that defeats the Christian Church. She's always been well-equipped to deal with death" (*Plays*, 317–18). Padre provides the requisite religious sentiments for the camp, as events require.

A third figure in Orton's trinity of authoritarians is the pieties-spouting Irish anarchist, Redcoat Riley, who takes over the duties of the deceased entertainments organizer. He conducts Erpingham's funeral at the end of the play with the same kind of insanity—four dozen red balloons to represent each year of Erpingham's life—with which he conducts the camp entertainment.

When Erpingham hands over to Riley the position of entertainments organizer, he does so with the usual motivational speech. To the music of "Land of Hope and Glory" Erpingham charges Riley with his duties in an oration of nationalistic clichés, which include the long-standing contempt for subjects in other lands, in this case, Ireland:

Tonight is your testing time. Let the spirit of Enterprise and Achievement go with you. Remember our Glorious Dead. How many soldiers have had tasks like yours? . . . The courage and grit that founded Empires still stands. And when, Riley, we plant our flag upon the white, untouched plains of Asia—you will be in our thoughts that day. The Camps of India, the Eternal Tents of the East will echo to your name. . . . And in those times we shall rejoice that, of your own free will, you were born an Englishman. (*Plays*, 288–89)

Riley, however, protests that he is an Irishman, only to be admonished by Erpingham that Ireland is counted as England and, furthermore, that Ireland should be content with its "empty roads, Galway Bay, and the remains of Sir Roger Casement" (*Plays*, 289). Riley, ever the survivor, retorts that these three qualifications are more than enough and that even with only two of them "we'd be a nation of poets and talkers still" (*Plays*, 289). A Sloane-type survivor, Riley accepts Erpingham's (and England's) authority as seen in his acceding to Erpingham's request to wear the badge of office.

The pageantry of England is satirized in Erpingham's fantasizing to Riley about his vision of an earthly paradise: "Rows of Entertainment Centres down lovely, unspoiled bits of the coast, across deserted moorland and barren mountainside." With the music of "The Holy City" accompanying his fantasy, Erpingham continues, "There'll be dancing. And music. Colourful scenes. Official pageantry. Trained drum Majorettes will march hourly across the greensward. The shapeliest girls in Britain—picked from thousands of disappointed applicants. There'll be no shortage of horses. And heated pools. The accommodation will be lavish. Slot machines will be employed for all tasks" (*Plays*, 282–83). Riley warns Erpingham of the possibility of Fortune's wheel bringing him down and supports his advice with the story of the sad fate of a nun who "itched like the Devil to become Mother Superior." Erpingham, however, dismisses the possibility as "Hibernian cant" (*Plays*, 282). In Orton's universe, Riley's acquiescence to Erpingham is not so much a matter of hypocrisy as it is the modus operandi of the survivalist among the welfare-state gentility. His warning to Erpingham reflects Orton's constant wariness about the critical and financial rewards he enjoyed with *Entertaining Mr. Sloane* and *Loot* after so many years of living on the dole and with literary failure.

When Riley warns Erpingham that the projection for a new camp involves National Trust territory that happens to be a bird sanctuary, Erpingham responds in the perversity of Ortonesque wit—that human beings as well as birds need sanctuaries and that Riley lacks the pioneering spirit.

Standard entertainments for the campers are special targets for Orton's wicked glee. At one point Erpingham announces over a loudspeaker to campers in their chalets the winners of the glamorous granny competition, the mother and child competition, and the disability bonus to a man whose legs were "certified 'absolutely useless by our Resident Medical Officer.' Yet he performed the Twist and Bossa Nova to the tune specified on the entrance form" (*Plays*, 283). A blind woman is cheered on by her audience as they help her locate her diving board. When Riley takes over as entertainments organizer, he asks for a volunteer to be the

weekly Tarzan of the Apes, whose role will be enacted in full costume—
the leopard skin. There will be, as well, the requisite beauty queen
parade.

It is but a short step from the rigid organization of these perversely
Edenic entertainments to total mayhem, and here the step is provoked
by a petty incident. The rabble is led by two couples: Kenny and Eileen,
who is incapable of stopping her incessant reminders to all that she is
pregnant and that her marriage had ostracized her from her family, and
Ted and Lou, who had met at gatherings of Young Conservatives, whom
Lou found to be "polite and sympathetic." In one of the games the par-
ticipant who can scream the loudest receives a week's groceries. A fight
breaks out, and Riley, perceiving Eileen to have lost control of herself,
slaps her. Kenny comes to his wife's rescue, calling Riley a pig for hitting
a pregnant woman. The melee grows, and in the midst of its escalation,
Erpingham, attempting to restore order, quotes from the Bible: "Blessed
are the Meek." He praises his priest who "has quelled the anger of the
politically unawakened. As the dove alighted on the Ark after the Flood,
bringing hope to those within, so too he settles our fears and calms our
troubled thoughts" (*Plays*, 314). His words are soon undercut by the
appearance of a battered Padre, and now Erpingham changes to a historical tune: "Twenty Christian Centuries in the Dust. The Devil's
Congress has belted the Lord's Annointed" (*Plays*, 315). But, in Orton's
words, life has begun to defeat Christianity as his efforts to contain the
rebellion become increasingly futile.

Mixing his parodic tragedy with burlesque of an epic tradition, Orton
has Erpingham convene a council of war to debate opposing strategies.
Riley proposes thrashing out the argument with the rebels over "a cup of
instant." The political and religious arguments of Riley and Padre favor
arbitration. Padre claims that if the pharoahs had followed his line of reasoning, the Egyptians would not have been afflicted with the 10 plagues.
Erpingham, however, recommends a rigid defiance of the forces of anarchy with all that is best in twentieth-century civilization—ignoring force
and doing nothing: "I shall put a record of Russ Conway on the gram
and browse through a James Bond" (*Plays*, 308). The rebels also have a
strategy meeting, with Ted arguing for reasonable action in accordance
with the law. Kenny, sounding very much like the Americans who defied
England in the eighteenth century, insists that in everyone's life there
comes a time when he must choose between being treated badly or taking "by force those common human rights which should be denied no
man" (*Plays*, 309).

The tumult reaches crisis proportions when Kenny slaps Erpingham, causing Padre, white-faced, to pronounce, "You've struck a figure of authority!" (*Plays*, 303). With falling plaster and blood around them, Riley, as he calls for the night porter's bicycle, recommends flight in the manner of Shakespeare's Richard III—if, that is, they can make it to the transport station. In the meantime violence reigns, sounding to Erpingham like the Devil's Mass. Erpingham is killed—his death the ritual death of the old king. He is Orton's mock version of Euripides' Pentheus, and the irrational events attendant on the denial of the Dionysian life force—parodically symbolized by Eileen's pregnancy—are Orton's revenge on authority.

That revenge is taken not only on government and religion, but also on the use of the arts for political purposes. Erpingham bemoans the lack of a national poet to record the violence that meets his eyes on entering the grand ballroom, a sight that included women's briefs on the stairs and the "hellish squadron," "half-naked spewing up their pork and beans" (*Plays*, 304). Padre reinforces Erpingham's lament with his likening of the mayhem to "an allegorical painting by one of the lesser Masters" (*Plays*, 305). The painting is *Christ Mocked*, which had hung in the Walker Art Gallery of Liverpool.

Joining literature and painting in Orton's satiric collage is a variety of classical and popular music heard throughout the play. Actions are matched with ironically appropriate music that intensifies the madness. "Le Marseillaise" punctuates the rebels' decision to fight, and Erpingham's funeral is duly accompanied with a choir's rendition of "The Holy City." Other popular patriotic and religious strains keep pace with the action: "Land of Hope and Glory," "Zadok the Priest and Nathan the Prophet Annointed the King," "Fold Your Wings of Love Around Me," "The Dead March" from *Saul*, "The Chinese Dance" from *The Nutcracker Suite*, "Love Divine All Loves Excelling," and Bach's "Toccata and Fugue." Music is important in Orton's use of Brechtian technique to parody conventions of the epic and tragic genres. He issues specific instructions that lighting and banners be used "after the manner of the Royal Shakespeare Company's productions of Shakespeare's plays" (*Plays*, 278). His war with the authorities of past and contemporary civilization—and a total war in its use of traditional techniques to parody themselves—results in an aesthetic self-demolition derby.

Similarly, Orton smashes hypocrisy in one very funny fusion of religion, politics, and sex. As Erpingham undresses he covers the portrait of the queen, even as he conducts a discussion with Padre about the subject of his next sermon, the Gadarene demoniac and the swine. Conceding its instructive value, he asks Padre for its meaning. Padre's response is that "we are meant to understand . . . that with madness, as with vomit, it's the passer-by who receives the inconvenience" (*Play*, 290). In response to a question about his interest in religion, Padre informs Erpingham that he is interested only from the "purely Christian point of view," finding "great solace in the life of the spirit" (*Plays*, 291). On the heels of that reply, Erpingham asks what happened in court that morning and is informed that Padre had been acquitted of sexual charges, made and then dropped, by a young woman. Properly costumed, Erpingham then directs Padre to uncover the queen's portrait, since he "can give her an audience now." The shedding and donning of costumes, the madness and talk of madness, and details such as the leopard skin worn by an inmate portraying Tarzan are only some of Orton's tricks that he reinvents in *What the Butler Saw*.

Orton's uniqueness remains his hilariously devastating wit—not yet in top form here, but effective still. It bears resemblance to the conceited style of seventeenth-century writers, defined by Samuel Johnson in the eighteenth century and then appropriated by T. S. Eliot in the twentieth century. In his essay "The Metaphysical Poets" Eliot quotes Johnson's definition of the conceit as "the most heterogeneous ideas . . . yoked by violence together."[1] Orton's use of the conceit as a weapon of farcical travesty may be different in aim from that of the seventeenth-century poets, but his violent yoking of widely disparate image and dialogue, one undercutting the other, results in the epigrammatic wit that is his Bacchic shout. Erpingham, for example, calls out for "a couple of verses of 'Love Divine All Loves Excelling,'" to be followed by "fire-hoses, tear-gas and the boot from then on" (*Plays*, 315). The shock value of Orton's brutally comic ending of *The Ruffian on the Stair*, according to Peter Gill after a conversation about Eliot with Orton and Kenneth Williams, does not exist for itself. Orton wanted "to force you to deliberately re-examine the structure—of language, of manners, of morals, of institutions. His instincts were always healthy" (Lahr 1978, 18).

Under the guise of observing due process of law, Padre organizes the official explanation of Erpingham's death. He recommends that the reporting of Erpingham's death to the police be like that of the apostles' memorable reply (not recorded in the Gospels) to a "Jerusalem J.P." to whom an account of Christ's disappearance had to be given. The biblical reply was a simple "He went up into the air." So must Erpingham's death be kept to a simple explanation: "He fell through the floor" (*Plays*,

318). The integrity of the camp must at all costs be preserved. The scene is reminiscent of Sergeant Truscott's manipulation of the truth in *Loot*. Later, in *What the Butler Saw*, psychiatrists and law officer similarly conspire to keep events out of the paper.

Yet even as this bit of corruption occurs, Kenny and other rebels pledge their anti-Erpingham solidarity. To them, Erpingham is still the bastard who insulted Eileen. They hope to find the police sympathetic, their reason being that "most of them [the police] have had their own wives insulted at some time or another" (*Plays*, 318).

The conceit is collectively illustrated in the screams of laughter on fun night in the grand ballroom that become one with screams of pain, as one camper bangs Riley in the groin with her handbag and another slaps Erpingham. The final scene in its apocalyptic nature looks forward to that of *What the Butler Saw*. Here red balloons, stained-glass windows, and strains of "The Holy City" surround the body of the dead Erpingham.

In its controlled chaos *The Erpingham Camp* moves beyond the personal and social morality of *The Ruffian on the Stair* and *Entertaining Mr. Sloane* to the level of farce in which morality has been totally depersonalized. In Orton's stage world all classes are criminal classes, no problem is solved, and there is no punishing of the comic villain; even Erpingham's death does not change things, for his successor will continue running the camp, with the help of Padre's lying about the death.

All characters are farcical stereotypes. Neither authorities nor rebels are exempt—the former as figures of greed and power and the latter as automatons of middle-class respectability. The highly organized holiday camp is Orton's disguise for contemporary England and its empty rituals carried on in the empty dialogue of the prevailing culture-speak. As a parody of *The Bacchae*, *The Erpingham Camp* is Orton's first direct, all-out satire on authority and, thus, his paean to anarchy. If *The Ruffian on the Stair* is prelude to *Entertaining Mr. Sloane*, *The Erpingham Camp* is forerunner of *What the Butler Saw*. As such, the collective title—*Crimes of Passion*—appropriately describes Orton's passion for the truth—one in the form of Wilson's personal revenge and the other the campers' collective revenge. Orton's need to rage for the humiliations and guilt imposed by authoritarian forces is his passion.

The first stage production of *Crimes of Passion* occurred only after *Entertaining Mr. Sloane* and *Loot* had become successes. *The Ruffian on the Stair*, written in 1963, had already undergone a radio airing; the BBC had published the radio version, and Orton rewrote it for an ITV production (temporarily deemed unfit for family viewing). In production notes Orton directs that "the author's extravagance of dialogue" not be matched "with extravagance of direction," as it "must be directed and acted with absolute realism" (Lahr 1978, 130). The blending of laughter and terror, however, was still not realized successfully. In a mixed review, Irving Wardle of the London *Times*, speaking to Orton's intent to blend violence and comedy, concluded that the "comedy is grossly outweighed by meaningless violence."[2] In its three versions (excluding its source, the novel *The Boy Hairdresser*) *The Ruffian on the Stair* elicited mixed reviews, similar to Wardle's—as a "first play" that contains basic thematic and stylistic qualities that appear in Orton's subsequent plays but fail to blend laughter and terror satisfactorily. As Peter Gill, director of the original stage version, noted, this remains Orton's only play in which "he tried to write about genuine homosexual emotions," never again to write "another play with emotions of this kind" (Lahr 1978, 134). Unlike Orton, whose loneliness and social inadequacy was assuaged by his writing and by what Lahr describes as "eerily anonymous" sexual encounters, Wilson has no such protection, and his recourse, like Hallowell's, is self-destruction.

The *Erpingham Camp*, however, generally recognized as Orton's best short play, received better notices than did *The Ruffian on the Stair*, with minor qualifications regarding the second half of the play in which the political significances obtruded too strongly on the farcical action. Still, as a "nightmare extravaganza of totalitarianism in a British holiday camp," it "offers some wicked parodies of holiday season shows, and a pair of richly droll performances by Roddy Maude-Roxby as the Irish Saboteur and Bernard Gallagher as the corseted dictator" (Wardle, 8).

As different as the two plays may be, they contain interestingly similar lines that express Orton's attempt to unsettle the audience with laughter and terror. In the earlier play, Mike's serious remark that the police will understand his shooting for "they have wives and goldfish of their own" (*Plays*, 61) parallels that of Kenny in *The Erpingham Camp* that the police, with wives of their own, will understand the death of Erpingham. One is rooted in terror and the second in laughter—an indication of Orton's progress toward a flawless blending of the two so successfully achieved in *What the Butler Saw*.

The mixed notices, following the strong success of *Entertaining Mr. Sloane*, prompted Orton to seek and find another of his anonymous Holloway Road sexual satisfactions, lengthily detailed in his *Diaries*, and then to travel to Tangier for his and Halliwell's last holiday.

Chapter Five

Passionless Crimes: *The Good and Faithful Servant* and *Funeral Games*

If passions, personal and public, reign in *The Ruffian on the Stair* and *The Erpingham Camp*, they are conspicuous by their absence in Orton's two other television plays—*The Good and Faithful Servant* (1964) and *Funeral Games* (1966). There is no life force to catalyze the action of either play, thus their pairing as plays about crimes without passion. There is only the author's own silent shout in one and his witty ferocity in the other.

In *The Good and Faithful Servant* there is the poignancy of Buchanan, whose cradle-to-grave security has its own traditional appeal. At no time, however, does he even question the authority that has shaped him into a member of Orton's welfare-state gentility. The saddest line in all of Orton's plays may be Buchanan's when, upon reaching retirement age after 50 years of working at the main entrance to the plant, he admits that nobody at his first get-together with the group of retired workers knows him or has even seen him before. The crime in this play is the firm's reduction of the worker to a nobody, yet Buchanan's silent complicity is also a crime.

In *Funeral Games*, the last of Orton's four short plays, institutional corruption is again in place, unsatisfyingly even for those who have become accustomed to Ortonesque style. The lives of two men of the cloth—the fraudulent Pringle and the defrocked McCorquodale, a wife murderer—are joined as the former employs a private detective to investigate the latter's suspected adultery with Pringle's wife and murder of his own wife. With its faint echoes of the revenge plot of *The Ruffian on the Stair*, the play exploits the subject of crime, but it does so with such total detachment that even the self-serving Inspector Truscott in *Entertaining Mr. Sloane* or Dr. Rance in *What the Butler Saw* seem at least human. Except for Tess, who is a re-creation of Joyce in *The Ruffian on the Stair*, there are no life forces to counter the detached criminality of the two clerics. A sick morbidity replaces the hilarity that would normally be the reaction in an Orton play to a cleric's threat of revenge when reporters accuse him of *not* murdering his wife. An attack on the hypocrisy of religion that has corrupted and made irrational its clergy, the play is redeemed by its abundance of wit, such as Pringle's assurances to his wife that she "will remain the wife of the Bishop of Bonnyface [Pringle's title]. . . . I'll confirm the appointment later" (*Plays*, 358).

Generally regarded as the least successful of Orton's plays, *Funeral Games* is a grotesque variation on *The Good and Faithful Servant*, as ferocious corruption replaces ironic sterility. A major stylistic difference from Orton's other plays is its unrelieved black humor. In place of the human elements in *The Ruffian on the Stair*, the hilarity of *The Erpingham Camp*, or the ironic sympathy for Buchanan—despite his acquiescence in his fate—in *The Good and Faithful Servant*, there is the total perversion of good and the absence of any character even faintly human, except, arguably, the social worker, Tess, whose powerlessness is reminiscent of that of Mr. McLeavy in *Entertaining Mr. Sloane*.

The Good and Faithful Servant

Written in 1964 and first aired on Rediffusion Television on 6 April 1967, *The Good and Faithful Servant* stands apart from Orton's other plays in both subject matter and style. In 19 scenes the play's events seem conventional on the surface and end with the requisite happy ending of the traditional comedy. All the loose ends of the life of George Buchanan are neatly tied together, involving even the correction of a mildly errant youthful sexual liaison. His life has been set in order, and he dies as quietly as he has lived, with his one moment of self-recognition—"Nobody knows me"—soon falling into place with the sense of resignation that has characterized his entire life.

Orton introduces his play with epigraphs from two authorities—the Bible and the *Concise English Dictionary*: "Well done, thou good and faithful servant" (Matthew 25:21), and the definition of faith—"Faith, n. reliance, trust, in; belief founded on authority." The quotations are contrapuntal to those about anarchy (from Shaw's *Misalliance*) with which he prefaces *Loot*. If *The Ruffian on the Stair* and *The Erpingham Camp* celebrate anarchy, *The Good and Faithful Servant* passionlessly indicts authority. Life breathes in the anarchy of *The Erpingham Camp* in the same degree to which it is suffocated in the obedient lives of *The Good and Faithful Servant*. The tone here is unrelievedly funereal as in no other

Orton play. The root cause is the cradle-to-grave security guaranteed the employees of a modern corporation.

The play begins with a coincidence on which the action is based. For the remaining 18 scenes the straightforward account of the events in George Buchanan's life until he dies is at odds with the strange situations that usually pack an Orton play, as in the suspenseful Pinteresque situations of his comedy of menace—*The Ruffian on the Stair*—or the madness of farces such as *The Erpingham Camp* or *Loot.* Traditional as well is Orton's use of coincidence, surprise, and discovery, all occurring in the first scene, following which there is an inexorably naturalistic movement toward the penultimate scene in which the retiree dies. Perhaps more un-Ortonesque than any other aspect of the play is its generation of sympathy rather than of detachment or alienation as in other Orton plays. The sympathy is in good part due to Orton's naturalistic dramatization of a commonplace series of events with which an ordinary audience can easily identify. Any laughter that accompanies those events is essentially sympathetic, and at its extreme only ironic.

The irony is established in the first scene and maintained without disruption to the end. The surprise revelations to George Buchanan on the day of his retirement from a paternalistic industrial firm seem, in Orton's telling, as ordinary as almost any event during the 50 years of his life with the firm. Buchanan takes the news in stride as he does the retirement rites through which he is carefully guided by the superbly efficient personnel manager, Mrs. Vealfoy. In fact, the secrets here are the only ones in the play, and the remaining scenes merely finish off with unsurprising detail a most unsurprising life. Buchanan, in beginning his prescribed rites of passage to old age, encounters a scrubwoman who, like himself, has worked for the firm for 50 years:

BUCHANAN: Is this the Personnel section?

EDITH: Yes.

BUCHANAN: I've found it at last. I've had a long journey.

EDITH: Are you expected?

BUCHANAN: Yes. I'm retiring today. They're making a presentation. I'm the oldest living employee. My photograph will be in the firm's magazine. They've already arranged the particulars. I gave them every assistance, of course. (*Edith wrings water from a cloth into a bucket.*) I recall them building this block. My

first day here coincided with the Foundation ceremony. (*Edith looks up*.)

EDITH: So did mine. I was crushed up against a wall by a
              section of the crowd. My mother complained on my
              behalf. But nothing official ever came of it.

BUCHANAN: How long have you worked here?

EDITH: Fifty years. I have breaks, of course. For pregnancy
              and the occasional death of a near relative.

BUCHANAN: I've been here for fifty years, too. How strange
              we've never met.

EDITH: Which gate did you use?

BUCHANAN: Number eight.

EDITH: Ah, well, you see, that explains it. I've always
              entered by number 15. (*Plays*, 153–54)

The numbness of the dialogue sets the tone for the play. In the rest of
the first scene Orton compresses a bizarre three-generational story set off
by Edith's memory being jogged by something familiar in Buchanan's
stance. Buchanan discovers that his youthful sexual escapade with Edith
had engendered twin boys who, prior to their identical deaths from
drinking water from a poisoned well, had shared sex with a "young girl
of impeccable character." To Buchanan's question about the father of the
resulting pregnancy, Edith replies, "No one knows" (*Plays*, 155).

The introductory scene resembles one from Eugène Ionesco's *The
Bald Soprano*, in which two very English couples, Mr. and Mrs. Martin
and Mr. and Mrs. Smith, discover by means of syllogistic logic that they
are married to each other. The sterility of their lives is the subject of
Ionesco's play, one of the major absurdist plays of the post–World War II
era. Ionesco's characters are farcical caricatures, whereas Orton's
Buchanan and Edith are realistically ordinary, having more in common
with Herman Melville's Bartleby and with Nicolai Gogol's Akakyevitch
Bashmachkin in "The Overcoat." Sympathy for Buchanan, like that for
Bartleby and Akaki, although occasionally interrupted by bits of poten-
tially farcical actions, keeps the rest of the play on the level of satirical
yet sympathetic humor rather than farce.

There is, for example, the scene in which Buchanan is given the requisite retirement gifts—a toaster and a clock. There is the ritual in which
he, behind a screen, sheds his uniform, piece by piece, handing it to a
man who then puts it on a dummy and wheels it away. Another scene

that would normally be grist for Orton's laughter mill—the toaster goes off with a flash and a bang when first put into use—is only one in a series of minor disasters in a long life. Edith's comment to Buchanan, who is "in a state," is that "we'll have to abandon my original plan of toast for tea" (*Plays*, 168). The clock also malfunctions, its hands moving backward rather than clockwise and giving Buchanan yet another shock.

Becoming depressed, he is hurried by Mrs. Vealfoy to the firm's recreation center. Here again there is the potential for the kind of farce so gleefully played out in *The Erpingham Camp*. Her antidote to the modern disease of depression is to get one's mind off one's self, as she points out to Buchanan the "dominoes, cards and darts and all the pastimes": "And over here we have conversation" (*Plays*, 183–84). The heart of this scene, and perhaps of the play, is the pervasive silence in the group when Mrs. Vealfoy asks for anyone who may remember him. Under pressure, one old man finally raises his hand. The ironic sympathy of the old man's "I was almost mentioned in a well-known sporting periodical once" (*Plays*, 185) is a prelude to Buchanan's "Nobody knows me. They've never seen me before" (*Plays*, 189). When asked by Mrs. Vealfoy what he was thinking just now, Buchanan says, "Nothing." Buchanan's nothingness includes his inability to join in the group singing since he did not know the words of the song. Mrs. Vealfoy coaxes him out of his mental blankness to hum with the group. The song, ironically, is "I Want to Be Happy."

Even Orton's signature burlesques of sexual mores are limited to two incidents—one involving Buchanan's youthful sexual miscreancy and the other a sharing by twin brothers of the same woman, resulting in the indeterminacy of the father of her child. These Orton treats as he does the clock and toaster—minor incidents and indiscretions rather than as farcical bits to flaunt his societal grievances. Both the typically bizarre behavior of characters and his artistically disjunctive wit and imagery are rare. Where they do exist, they operate in a vacuum. The void outside the characters matches their inner voids, leaving no room for self-awareness, let alone rebellion or anarchy, to endow them with a sense of life.

Fodder for Orton's satire of Buchanan's quiescence to the firm's regulation of his life permeates the play, as in his unquestioning acceptance of his separation rites. Mrs. Vealfoy instructs him about leaving with "no unpaid debts, no arrears of credit" and about such minutiae as leaving his clock card, "overalls, boots, gloves and any other equipment or clothing belonging to the firm by 3:20" (*Plays*, 157). She then recognizes his "losing a limb in the service of the firm. You conceal your disabilities well" (*Plays*, 157). She then warns him that "we are in no way responsible for your other limbs. If they deteriorate in any way the firm cannot be held responsible" (*Plays*, 158). The satiric thrust sharpens with Buchanan's informing Mrs. Vealfoy about his just having "learned of a descendant of whom I had no knowledge" (*Plays*, 159), that descendant being Ray, his and Edith's grandson. The information promptly sets in motion Mrs. Vealfoy's arranging of a job for Ray, his marriage to Debbie, and the booking of a place for their forthcoming child in the firm's nurseries.

In contrast, Mrs. Vealfoy is unflagging in her optimism. Maurice Charney considers her the main character, rather than Buchanan. She is zealous in her instruction to Ray, Buchanan's grandson, to say "'yes' as often as possible" (*Plays*, 181). She intends to wean him from his current drift in life by giving him some direction. Her authority over him is religious as she asks him whether he feels he has done any wrong in impregnating Debbie. As personnel manager-social worker, Mrs. Vealfoy is high priestess of the new sociopsychological religion. Rather than admonishing Ray when he admits no guilt, she accedes to his wish to marry Debbie with a jargonized rejoinder: "I always like the end achieved to coincide with established practice, though the means to the end may vary with custom" (*Plays*, 182).

Mrs. Vealfoy, however—although bearing the brunt of Orton's ironic thrusts at corporate cradle-to-grave paternalism, and, as well, that of England as a welfare state—is not an entirely unsympathic figure in her role as the sterile proprietress of sterile lives. The implementing arm of her firm, she, like Erpingham, controls the lives of her clients. The difference between the two is striking in the scene at the recreation center in which planned entertainment is provided for the retirees. Mrs. Vealfoy has no selfish or devious purpose in the execution of her duties, as does the greedy Erpingham in his holiday camp or Nurse Fay in her attempts to manage the McLeavy family in *Entertaining Mr. Sloane*. Unlike the other characters in the play, she is energetic in the pursuit of employees' welfare, and she lives as a dramatic character as the others do not. Her managerial energy and vibrancy stand out from the unthinking pliancy of those whose lives she manages.

The play in some ways is a companion piece to *The Erpingham Camp*— both plays being allegories for Orton's view of contemporary England, yet in completely obverse styles. Both deal with the abuse of personal identities by prevailing authorities.

The title, with its biblical roots, illustrates yet again Orton's famous line in *The Erpingham Camp* that life, always equipped to deal with death, defeats the Christian church, with the firm here being a secular replacement for the church. Sterility remains unchallenged by Orton's usual rebels who upset or demolish authority. In Orton's perversely happy ending for Buchanan, he dies quietly shortly after the marriage of Ray and Debbie and just before the annual employee get-together gets under way. He dies without any self-awareness, even his errant youth a part of the routine nature of his life. No satyr romps in this ironic comedy, and no anarchic spirit even attempts the overthrow of authority and its symbols. The play's passivity is only intensified in the creation of a situation that normally would be ripe for Ortonesque anarchy. The three-generational tale of illegitimate births, the sexual sharing of one woman by twin brothers, incest and homosexuality—all these take on the routine quality of the clock-and-toaster retirement ritual.

More fully than in any other Orton play, Buchanan is Orton's fictional rendition of the nature of his own father. He is a completely realized character, as the fathers in *Entertaining Mr. Sloane* and *Loot* are not. The play seems an exorcism of Orton's nonrelationship with a father he never really knew. It is a perverse paean to William Orton, who spent his entire life quietly, removed from any emotional interest except his lifelong gardening for the city of Leicester. Orton never visited his father in the retirement home in which he spent his last years. The explanation for the drearily absurdist tone of the play may lie in Orton's inability to render his father as an object of laughter.

Lahr writes of the "seething disgust" of *The Good and Faithful Servant* and of "the blast of the irony . . . muted by the naturalistic format." He regards the play as Orton's compulsion "to exhibit his mastery of the dead world . . . in a style as extreme as his own success." The "threat of anonymity, the suffocating memory of his upbringing, and [his] literary failures were symbolic deaths from which Orton now drew power for life" (Lahr 1978, 186). Orton's resurrection from this sense of death is witnessed in his next play, *Loot*.

Funeral Games

Written in 1966, between *Loot* and *What the Butler Saw, Funeral Games* was first aired posthumously by Yorkshire Television on 25 August 1968 as part of an ITV series, "The Seven Deadly Virtues." The series title could hardly be more Ortonesque. The irony is doubled in the choice of

subject for Orton's contribution—charity. Lahr regards *Funeral Games* as
a "transitional play between *Loot* and *What the Butler Saw* in which
Orton tried to solidify the stylistic advances of language and logic in
Loot." In fact, *Funeral Games*, Orton's original choice as a title for *Loot*,
was changed at the urging of Halliwell. The cast of the television production included Vivien Merchant—at the time the wife of Harold
Pinter—an accomplished actress who had acted successfully in many of
her husband's plays.

With its echoes of the revenge plot of Orton's first and most
Pinteresque play, *The Ruffian on the Stair, Funeral Games* has its own distinction as Orton's most grotesque drama. The revenge plot hinges on
the efforts of one clergyman to investigate a rumor of his wife's infidelity
and then later to murder her. A second cleric, upon discovering his wife's
affair, had beaten her to death and then buried her in the basement of
their home. The paths of the two clerics cross as each discovers that his
wife had been involved in some way with the other. Religion, heretofore
only one of many targets of Orton's satire, now occupies center stage in
a no-holds-barred unleashing of a relentlessly freakish series of actions
and even more ingeniously freakish twists of logic that leap from their
comparatively mild nature in *Loot* to a lunacy that Orton later executes
to near-perfection in *What the Butler Saw*. The characters are totally
divorced from any semblance of humanity. Their dialogue, in the con-
torted and distorted turns and twists of logic, takes on a life of its own,
making both the characters and their behavior clearly an excuse for the
complete license Orton takes with language. The artistic detachment
Orton had begun in prison reaches ebullient heights during a time of
fast-mounting stage successes. Literally, language is all as both characters and plot, for all their melodramatic criminality, are gradually
absorbed into the tortuously labyrinthine paths of the logic of Pringle
and McCorquodale.

Pringle is the leader of a sect called The Brotherhood, who "hang
about on street corners" and have a house of contemplation in the
Arcade (*Plays*, 323). McCorquodale is a defrocked priest who had been
undone by a bishop whose "name in religion" (a Pinteresque turn of
phrase that is later used in regard to McCorquodale) is Goodheart.
McCorquodale later discovers that Pringle is Bishop Goodheart and that
his (McCorquodale's) health worker, Tessa, is Pringle's wife.

The grotesque events begin in the opening scene with Pringle's interviewing of Caulfield, who is applying for a position as private investigator. The similarity to the opening scene of *What the Butler Saw* is seen in

the bizarre comments of the interview. Pringle orders Caulfield to "sit down. Or kneel if you'd prefer. I want you to behave naturally" (*Play*, 323). In one of the many tales of sexual miscreancy by the two clerics, Pringle quizzes Caulfield regarding his success at controlling himself. Caulfield claims success just before Christmas, to which Pringle replies with a reference to Christmas as the "Festival of the Renewal of the Spirit. . . . We have a cot with a baby in it outside the church. I dare say you're surprised by the unusualness of the conception" (*Plays*, 324). The line reworks the phrasing of Eddie's words to Kath in *Entertaining Mr. Sloane*—that it is only proper that "the dad is present at the conception" (*Plays*, 149). When Caulfield asks about payment, Pringle offers "a personal invitation to my exhibition of biblical documents. It's preceded by tea" (*Plays*, 326).

This diabolical unleashing of verbal wit feeds on itself, eventually relegating the physical action of the play to secondary importance. Pringle offers Caulfield the hospitality of chewing "a bit of root I dug up in the garden of Gethsemane" (*Plays*, 323) and, taking a flask from the cupboard, "a bottle of water here from the Well at Bethsaida" (*Plays*, 324). He himself uses its miraculous powers as a laxative. He directs Pringle to report on the morrow, as "my candle burns until the third cock crow" (*Plays*, 326). Pringle's piety is demonstrated in the shape of his hot water bottle—a cross. Religious ritual is turned on its head as, for example, in McCorquodale's still wearing a "dog-collar" from force of habit and to keep warm. He remarks on the bad legs he had suffered for years "after I was forced to give up the Roman skirt" (*Plays*, 327).

Obsessed with investigating his wife, Tessa, who is a social worker, Pringle fuels his skewed logic into concluding that public sentiment will be on his side if he can prove her infidelity. Furthermore, the publication of the scandal could prove financially rewarding, with the money to be channeled to his religious organization. Valerie, McCorquodale's wife, now buried "under a ton of smokeless" (*Plays*, 331) in the basement, had been Tessa's friend, possibly her lover, as well as Pringle's. The situation of Pringle, McCorquodale, and Tessa adds up roughly to that of Wilson, Joyce, and Mike in *The Ruffian on the Stair*. At the end, Pringle and McCorquodale, with their accomplices, Tess and Caulfield, are led off to prison, with Tessa and Caulfield as accessories. Pringle utters the last words: "Let us go to prison. Some angel will release us from our place of confinement. . . . Everything works out in accordance with the divine Will" (*Plays*, 360). His words echo those of Dr. Rance at the conclusion of *What the Butler Saw*: "Let us put our clothes on and face the world" (*Plays*, 448).

The catalyst in the plot is Caulfield's job as investigator changing to one of possible murderer after Pringle's covenant with the Lord, who has appeared to him in the garden of the Lady of the Wand: "I was swept up and the springs of my heart were opened. I made a vow. Taking my cue from Holy Writ. 'My wife must be punished.' . . . The grounds of that Surrey mansion were ablaze with the ecumenical spirit until the wee hours. My commandment was repeated like a catechism: 'Thou shalt not suffer an adultress to live'" (*Plays*, 336). When Caulfield reminds Pringle of the Sixth Commandment, Pringle's logic takes over: "If she can break the seventh, I can break the sixth. Open that drawer. You'll find a gun" (*Plays*, 336).

Faced with the necessity of providing evidence of his wife's misbehavior, Pringle sends Caulfield to McCorquodale's home, where he discovers Valerie's dead body and from it cuts off a hand to bring in a tin to Pringle as proof. There is the added detail of Caulfield's acquiring Valerie's watch, which he claims fell from her severed hand: "No proper support, see" (*Plays*, 348). When Tessa discovers the contents of the tin, she gasps with fright: "A human hand in a Dundee cake tin" (*Plays*, 350).

Pringle uses the hand as faked evidence that he has murdered his wife but shrinks when Caulfield at one point confronts him with a gun that he (Caulfield) could use to murder Tessa. Pringle's logic springs to his defense:

> PRINGLE: I've already killed her once, I couldn't do it again. I'd be a murderer. . . .
>
> CAULFIELD: Unless you kill your wife, she'll accuse you of not being her murderer. (*Plays*, 353)

The twists of logic here resemble the argument in *What the Butler Saw* about whether one can have murdered someone who does not exist.

The most ingenious turn of logic involves Pringle's plan, agreed to by the other three, that Valerie's corpse be identified as Tessa's body and that Tessa be identified as McCorquodale's dead wife, Valerie. Ergo, the conspiracy has proved, to Pringle's satisfaction, that he is *not* innocent. His reputation as a wronged husband is preserved on the theory that even a cleric can be human. The wickedly ironic claim to humanity is all the more freakish for his total divorce from that very humanity as he exercises his religious authority in his varied sexual undertakings.

What happens between the initial scene of Pringle's interview with Caulfield and the last, in which police officers arrive, is the Black Mass—a total perversion of good, but a perversion whose mocking laughter, however darkly surrealistic, is Orton's honing of skills that he practices triumphantly in *What the Butler Saw*. Although no murder is committed in the course of the play, the devilishly distorted logic by which Pringle proceeds with his intentions constitutes the crime. The premise from which his actions stem is that "if my wife is committing adultery, my position would be intolerable. Being completely without sin myself I'd have to cast the first stone. . . . I make no secret of my views" (*Plays*, 326). The behavior of Pringle is surpassed in its offense to audience sensibilities by the familiar axioms in which the shocking actions are clothed.

A detail found in the earlier *Ruffian on the Stair* is Caulfield's breaking into McCorquodale's residence. He announces himself to McCorquodale as having "broken into your house"; the latter responds not with surprise but with a question about the manner of his entry: "Did you force a window?" (*Plays*, 329). After a discussion of the worm-eaten timbers, like McCorquodale's own ailing body, Caulfield, ironically, warns him about offering hospitality to rough young men who might terrorize him. His warning, however, is ignored as McCorquodale continues to offer him hospitality, even providing Caulfield with an explanation for his murder of his wife, Valerie. At a salvationist's meeting he had found "Bishop Goodheart—calling to order a number of female penitents on a straw mattress," of whom Valerie was one, "standing in her true colours. And very little else. . . . Up to the Devil's tricks. And he was up to hers. Oh, the Bacchic hound!" (*Plays*, 332). Following this experience, McCorquodale "learned to accept the irrational in everyday life" (*Plays*, 332) and to see that "all classes are criminal today. We live in an age of equality" (*Plays*, 333).

The ingenious twist in the story begins when a crime reporter insists on proof of a murder or else he would have to report Pringle's innocence. Pringle threatens to sue for defamation of character. When he realizes that he must provide evidence of the murder, Caulfield suggests the kinds of evidence needed: blood, a body, or at least an arm or a head. "Where could I get a head?" questions Pringle. "Even Harrods wouldn't accept the order" (*Plays*, 346). He finds that evidence and explains why he came up with only a hand. "I couldn't get her head off. It must be glued on." To Caulfield's comment McCorquodale adds, "She was always a headstrong woman" (*Plays*, 348). The ghoulish hand is one of Orton's farcical tricks with body parts, like the false teeth and eye in *Loot* and the Churchillian phallus in *What the Butler Saw*.

Like Mrs. Vealfoy in *The Good and Faithful Servant*, Tessa is the efficient and sympathetic institutional provider of health services for McCorquodale, and like Nurse Fay in *Loot*, she joins in the games, suggesting to Pringle that to save face he could pretend to murder her. Then, she contends, she "could stay here with my elderly gentleman [McCorquodale]" (*Plays*, 340). With Pringle and Caulfield, she contemplates the various forms her "death" could take. Although it isn't the kind of death she had hoped for, she considers their suggestion of a trip to Australia and, after a decent interval, to be "swept out to sea on a rubber raft," provided that she "was fully dressed and had recently attended some place of worship" (*Plays*, 340–41).

Later, tied up with rope by McCorquodale as the result of her threat to go to the police with information about Valerie's murder, she distracts him by encouraging him in his sentimental account of his life. With scissors from a trunk that was to be her coffin, she cuts herself free. Noting the mementos he lifts from the trunk, one of these a framed picture, to him a symbol of the Christian church, she offers, "A bird of prey carrying an olive branch. You've put the matter in a nutshell" (*Plays*, 355). The juxtaposition of vulture with dove is an appropriate metaphor for all of Orton's criminals, including the two clerics. In *Loot* police inspector and nurse join the two thieves in sharing the loot; all four here join forces to prevail in their lie to police that the woman in the cellar is Pringle's murdered adulteress wife and that Tessa is McCorquodale's wife. Pringle thus has saved himself from possible defamation by the press. He is vindicated in his claim as murderer of his wife. His potential financial gain is ensured, so he thinks.

Of Orton's four short plays, *Funeral Games*, in its grotesquerie, stands apart from the Pinteresque, highly personal revenge melodrama of *The Ruffian on the Stair*, the sympathetic satire of *The Good and Faithful Servant*, or the Bacchic celebration of anarchy in *The Erpingham Camp*. Its ghoulish stick figures, with the minor exception of Tessa whose thin claim to the human community is her insistent loyalty to Valerie, lack the life of a Wilson, Mike, and Joyce; the ironic sympathy of Buchanan and Mrs. Vealfoy; or the hilariously human criminality of Erpingham, Riley, and Padre.

Yet the wit in itself is sufficient reason for the play. Free-floating, the macabre wit seems disembodied from the characters, who themselves are divorced from any innocence that is in some form present in Orton's other work. At this high point in his career, Orton's holiday of devastating wit illustrates the achieved detachment in his art toward which he had worked throughout his career. Its very excess, however, only emphasizes the absence of the energizing passions that could have given the play the vibrancy found in his other plays. Instead of passions, the logical process accompanied by the famous Ortonesque epigrammatic perversion of commonplaces gives the play a satiric edge, Swiftian in its total disgust with humanity.

Chapter Six
Entertaining Mr. Sloane

Conscious of the similarities of his plays to Pinter's, Orton's agent, Peggy Ramsay, hesitated to sell *Entertaining Mr. Sloane* for fear that critics would label it "Pinterish" (*Diaries*, 14). Although the resemblances to Pinter in the earlier but as yet unproduced *Ruffian on the Stair* are unmistakable, they exist only superficially in both plot and characters in this, his first long stage play.

At first glance, similarities to three of Pinter's early plays—*The Room, The Birthday Party*, and *The Caretaker*—seem striking. In all three an unexpected visitor menacingly intrudes on the domesticity of a household of middle-aged couples (in the first two) and a tenement caretaker (in the last mentioned). So does Sloane, Orton's hero, but he arrives by invitation. Additional similarities to other characters appear and then dissipate. Mick, in *The Caretaker*, is an absentee landlord as is Eddie in Orton's play. Mick's brother Aston occupies his tenement house as caretaker, and Eddie's sister and father reside in the family home. Both look in on their respective households from time to time. When the intruder Davies appears in Pinter's play, he pits Aston against Mick and then Mick against Aston, just as Sloane plays daughter against father and then sister against brother. Sloane in some ways has more in common with Mick than with the intruder Davies, as he not only is provided with the room and board of his hostess but, like Mick in the earlier play, enjoys luxuries such as the feel of leather pants next to his skin. Like Mick, he is the antihero of the 1960s, the marginal man who a decade later follows the cultural exile, Jimmy Porter, famous for shaking the English stage world with his masochistic bursts of anger at the absence of great causes in the 1950s. Sloane, however, is no disillusioned idealist.

Similarities to Pinter's intruders fade quickly as the new antihero's survival skills are exercised. Like Orton himself, Sloane, according to Patrick Drumgoole, director of the original production, is a charmer and manipulator with the "almost godly posture of the true ironist who genuinely finds most things funny" (Lahr 1978, 149). Clearly unlike Pinter's intruders, Sloane is no threat, and the dislocating, Kafkaesque menaces of Pinter are conspicuous by their absence in Sloane. Instead he becomes established as a member of the family, and as such even his murder of the father, Kemp, is accepted by the family and will go unpunished by the law.

Another character, Eddie's middle-aged sister, Kath, has echoes of Pinter's middle-aged women. Her mother-whore need of Sloane parallels Meg Boles's attraction to a young lodger in *The Birthday Party*. Kath also bears a faint resemblance to Rose Hudd in *The Room*, the awakening of whose sexual past is the result of an intruder's presence. Rose's memories are fragmentary, whereas Kath's reminiscence of her youthful escapade that resulted in the birth of an illegitimate son is only another of Orton's many satirical thrusts at the destructive stigmas of middle-class life. Unlike the enigmatic nature of Meg and Rose, Kath is naturalistically developed, a creature of physical appetite and awareness of neighbors' gossip. For her, Sloane is a necessity, in contrast with Meg and Rose, for whom Stanley and Riley are, respectively, a playful diversion and a threat. Maurice Charney writes of Orton's ruthlessly cutting away of "Pinter's 'significances,' so that comedy of menace would seem a pretentious and misguided term for Orton's savage, anarchic and turbulent farces of daily life and empty deceptions" (Charney, 71). In subsequent plays Orton does away with even the surface resemblances to Pinter's characters and plots.

Unlike those of Pinter, Orton's character motivations are clear from the start—survival by whatever means necessary. For Kath, it is the primal mother-whore needs denied her by her stifling lower-middle-class environs. For Sloane, his good looks and physically fit body are the passage to the good life—a comfortable existence in which food, clothes, and use of a car are payment for his bisexual services. His current situation merely continues a pattern that began in his days in an orphanage. For Eddie, the surfaces of middle-class propriety are to be kept, despite the hinted-at impropriety of his business and his homosexuality. Kath's sexual indiscretions and Sloane's murders are the problems to which, as head of the household, he must give the proper appearances.

Entertaining Mr. Sloane, instead, is a lower-middle-class comedy of manners, whose key, John Russell Taylor writes, "is to be found in the strange relationship between the happenings of his plays and the manner in which the characters speak of them."[1] Thus one finds throughout Orton's work an Orwellian culture-speak like that of Eddie in his trivialization of a famous Dantean line— "He abandoned hope when he entered there"—in regard to Kath's oedipal behavior with Sloane.

The play is one long series of verbal confrontations, first between Kemp (the father) and Sloane; then between Eddie (the brother) and Sloane; and, finally, between Eddie and Kath, as each bargains for sexual rights to Sloane. The linguistic contests are characterized by misquotations and misapplied axiomatic sentiments in defense of socially indefensible actions. Orton dramatizes the "surrealistic dislocation between the most extraordinary and improper happenings and the unruffled propriety of the characters' conversation . . . held in perfect balance" (Taylor, 129).

Recommended to Michael Codron, artistic director of the New Arts Theater and the first producer of Pinter plays, by Peggy Ramsay on the word of John Tydeman, producer of *The Ruffian on the Stair* for BBC, the play brought Orton a success that changed his personal fortunes overnight at a time when he was living on a weekly government dole of about three pounds. Produced in 1964 in the middle of a decade of worldwide social upheaval, it captures the amorality of the times, but not in terms of the turbulent events of the times. Rather, Orton's world is restricted to the everyday lives of the lower-middle classes, and his satirical target is their use of respectable speech to disguise behavior at odds with the sentiments of that speech. Creating fresh epigrammatic wit from the sterility of existing axioms, Orton was hailed by Terence Rattigan as a dramatist "who had to say about England and society [what] had never been said before" in a society "diminished by telly technology . . . [where] everybody expresses themselves as if they were brought up on television" (quoted in Lahr 1978, 153).

Harold Pinter, himself a linguistic virtuoso, found Orton's work "brilliant and truly original."[2] Taylor regarded the play as "epoch making" and Orton as "finally, inimitable" in this the "first solid, well-managed commercial play which belongs, specifically and unmistakably to the post-Osborne era" (Taylor, 140). It is this inimitability that evoked the strong admiration of contemporary dramatists such as Rattigan and Pinter and of critics such as Taylor, Ronald Bryden, and Hilary Spurling. The play captures the amorality of the times out of which Orton wrote a "myth of society's ugliness" in order to expose that myth (Lahr 1978, 148).

The plot is simple and moves swiftly, containing little motivation for actions other than primal sexual needs. The language of prevailing mores and morality becomes a convenient disguise for the instinctive needs that drive a dysfunctional, lower-middle-class family. Kemp (Dadda) is the retired father, once gardener to a murdered pornographic photographer whose murderer he quickly identifies as Sloane. Kemp has

not spoken to his son, Eddie, for 20 years—since the day he had discovered him at the age of 17 "committing some kind of felony in the bedroom" (*Plays*, 71). His unwed, nymphomaniac daughter, Kath, now in
her forties, has lived for many years with the personal tragedy and social
stigma of an illegitimate child who was given out for adoption. Her
brother, Eddie, keeps the family comfortably well-off of by means of a
murkily referred-to "business," and he visits the family at regular inter-
vals. Their home is located near a dump, which, the father explains, was
the first in what was to be a row of houses, a project abandoned for lack
of funds.

The pivotal object in the setting of *Entertaining Mr. Sloane* is the set-
tee, on which Kath seduces Sloane in act 1, behind which Sloane kicks
Kemp's body at the end of act 2, and on which Kath, her father dead
and Sloane gone, sits, pregnant and alone, at the end of act 3. With the
idea for the plot first drawn from the brother-father relationship of
Oedipus at Colonus, Orton originally ended the play with the murder of
the father. He later moved the murder to its place in the second act, thus
bringing the character of the murderer-intruder, Sloane, as a combination of innocence and amorality, more sharply into focus. The plot construction is a conventional one, with each of the acts ending in a
cliffhanger that anticipates the changed relationships at the conclusion.
As Sloane and Eddie depart, the image that remains seems a burlesque
of the ending of Sartre's *No Exit*, in which three characters are
inescapably tied together for eternity. For Sloane and Eddie, the possibility of escape remains, but for Kath the double bind of dependence and
respectability offers little such hope.

The play's action begins with Kath's bringing home Sloane, whom
she had met at the library (and thus identified as cultured) and who is
about the same age as the son she was forced to give up. Even as she
insists on being Sloane's "mamma" and seeing to his material needs, she
dresses in a see-through robe and constantly comments on the smooth-
ness of Sloane's skin. As her intimacies with Sloane increase, Kemp's hostility toward the lodger becomes more pronounced. Despite his failing
eyesight, he recognizes Sloane as the murderer of his former employer
and threatens to expose him.

When Eddie appears for his visit, he, too, is hostile to Sloane's presence. He reminds Kath of her having scandalized the neighbors years
ago. After an exchange of Pinteresque questions and answers, however,
he finds himself attracted to the lodger and makes his own arrangements
with him, hiring him first as a chauffeur and then appropriating him as

a live-in mate. Hostilities between Kemp and Sloane reach a crisis point in a physical struggle in which Kemp dies, even as Kath and Eddie maneuver over possession of Sloane. The death serves as the catalyst for the resolution of the complications: Kath's problems with her pregnancy and neighborhood gossip, Sloane's murders and his need for a comfortable life, and Eddie's own sexual needs. Additionally, the death solves Eddie's problem of having to extract a signature from his stubborn father who refuses to sign the papers for admission to a home for the elderly.

The scanty plot belies the complex machinations of all three characters to effect their survivals on a variety of levels—sexual, personal, social, and moral. Orton intended Sloane as the pivotal character in the play and commented, in a letter to Alan Schneider, director of the New York production, on the simultaneously funny and alarming sexual stalking of Sloane by Kath and Eddie. He explains that Sloane knows that Eddie wants him, and "he has no qualms about surrendering his body" (*Plays*, 16). As a result, Sloane is able, at least temporarily, to be in control of the relationships. Orton further stated that he intended him as a bisexual charmer whom it takes Eddie some time to see for the natural survivor that he is. It is not until Eddie engages in a series of cat-and-mouse Pinteresque interrogations of Sloane that he realizes the full extent of Sloane's amoral nature. When he does, he is able, in the name of decency and respectability, to manipulate the proper survival of all three—himself, Sloane, and Kath—in the comic ending of the play.

In a series of minor power plays by Sloane and major ones by Eddie are superficial evocations of Pinteresque situations, but these exist primarily to advance Orton's satire of the disparity between scandalous actions and respectable speech rather than as enigmatic indications of complex psychological states, as is the case with Pinter's characters.

For example, in reproaching Kath for taking on a lodger, Eddie voices his concerns about appearances, suddenly ending his litany with a personal question that pierces the dead language:

You've got to realize my position. I can't have my sister keeping a common kip. Some of my associates are men of distinction. They think nothing of tipping a fiver. That sort of person. If they realized how my family carry on I'd be banned from the best places. (*Pause.*) And another thing . . . you don't want them talking

about you. An' I can't guarantee my influence will keep them quiet. Noisy neighbors and the scandal. Oh, my word, the looks you'll get. (*Pause.*)
How old is he? (*Plays*, 82)

Eddie has begun the positioning of himself in the acquisition of power
over Sloane, who with chameleonlike adaptability surrenders naturally to
whatever demands the situation makes on him. Eddie's early view of
Sloane as "a nice kid" and a "virgin," according to Orton, soon changes
(*Plays*, 16). He reinforces his appeal to Kath to avoid family scandal by
reminding her of her relationship many years ago with his mate, Tommy,
the result being her earlier pregnancy and the spoiling of a relationship
between Eddie and Tommy. Eddie's convincing argument is countered
with Kath's disguising of her need of Sloane in the axioms of familial
respectability. She claims Sloane's trustworthiness, witnessed in his
account of his monthly visitations to his parents' graves. The impact of
her emotional plea—the kind that Orton deals with as pure farce in *Loot*
and *What the Butler Saw*—is here both disconcerting and comic, a sub-
dued example of the kind of double effect—laughter and horror—toward
which Orton self-admittedly worked and which he realized increasingly
with every play: "He's trustworthy. Visits his parents [i.e., their graves]
once a month. Asked me to go with him. You couldn't object to a visit to
a graveyard? The sight of the tombs would deter my looseness. . . . He
hasn't any mamma of his own. I'm to be his mamma. He's an orphan.
Eddie, he wouldn't do wrong. Please don't send him away" (*Plays*, 83).

Her pleading is fruitless, and Eddie's maneuvering for control of the situation focuses on Sloane in Pinteresque interrogations that move inexorably
toward his seduction of Sloane and the determination of Kath's fate:

ED: You're fond of swimming?
SLOANE: I like a plunge now and then.
ED: Bodybuilding?
SLOANE: We had a nice little gym at the orphanage. Put me
          in all the teams they did. Relays . . . (*Ed looks interest-
          ed.*) . . . soccer . . . (*Ed nods.*) . . . pole vault, . . . long
          distance . . . (*Ed opens his mouth.*) . . . 100 yards, dis-
          cus, putting the shot. (*Ed rubs his hands together.*) Yes.
          Yes. I'm an all rounder. A great all rounder. In any-
          thing you care to mention. Even in life. (*Plays*, 86)

The exchange intensifies as Ed, breathless, questions Sloane about his exercising, reaching the kind of fantasy levels associated with the characters in Pinter's plays (e.g., Stanley's recital of his piano-playing achievements in *The Birthday Party*):

SLOANE:	As clockwork.
ED:	Good, good. Stripped?
SLOANE:	Fully.
ED:	Complete. . . . How invigorating.
SLOANE:	And I box. I'm a bit of a boxer.
ED:	Ever done any wrestling?
SLOANE:	On occasions.
ED:	So, so.
SLOANE:	I've got a full chest. Narrow hips. My biceps are—
ED:	Do you wear leather . . . next to the skin? Leather jeans, say? Without . . . aah . . .
SLOANE:	Pants? (*Plays*, 86–87)

The seduction of Sloane by Eddie allows Orton a logical progression to an arrangement by which Eddie's power over both Kath and Sloane solves the domestic, sexual, and legal problems for all three. Eddie extends his possession of Sloane to exclusive rights in warning him against the casual "bunking up" that goes on nowadays: "Too many lads being ruined by birds. I don't want you messing about with my sister" (*Plays*, 87).

These passages provide only a taste of the polite morality within which all three encase their instinctive, socially anarchic desires—for Sloane, a comfortable life, bisexual if necessary; for Kath, her oedipal needs; and, for Eddie, his homosexuality. When they must, all three lie to each other about themselves, as in the details of Kath's early pregnancy and of Sloane's two murders. Survival in a given situation dictates what is said, whether it is Sloane's security in the household, Kath's sexual needs, or Eddie's sexual inclinations. Nature, taking the form of sexuality in Orton's plays, is protean in her stratagems, shifting constantly to accommodate unexpected circumstances. The disguising of natural instincts in ludicrously inappropriate sentiments is not a matter of right or wrong but of momentary necessity. The disguises are aimed at destroying, not correcting, the institutionalized attitudes that foster hypocrisy and intolerance.

Of the quartet of characters, only Kemp retains conventional moral and societal underpinnings. He insists on identifying Sloane as the murderer of his former boss, despite Sloane's insistent attempts to convince him that the murder was a defensive act in response to shady goings-on. Kemp thus remains a threat to Sloane. He has never forgotten Eddie's youthful bedroom felony, presumably a homosexual act, as a result of which he had removed the lock from his son's door. Drawn partly from Orton's own father, he is, like Orton's father, a gardener and, again like Orton's father, uncommunicative. He speaks not at all to Eddie and only minimally to Kath, primarily about physical necessities.

Stifling in her attention to the details of domestic routines, the mothering of Sloane, and the avoiding of scandal, Kath, similarly, is patterned after Orton's mother, who took inordinate pains to keep her physical attractiveness and who once took in a lodger, paying what seemed to her children as disproportionate attention to him. Kath is overly protective of Sloane and constantly calls his attention to her attire. She offers Sloane a litany of amenities that include the use of the living room, the availability of aspirins, his choice of "flock or foam rubber" in his pillow, and a general welcome to him to be one of the family. Offering him a bath and calling to his attention that she is "rude" under her dress, something she says he probably has noticed, she easily proclaims her intentions. She sympathetically senses an "air of lost wealth" about Sloane and is appropriately shocked at his account of his parents passing away together, possibly in a suicide pact. She attempts an appeal to his sympathy in her tale of her illegitimate son's father, whose duty to his family kept him from marrying her. She does not answer the doorbell even now, for fear of the potential scandal by a gossipy neighbor who could be ringing it. Encasing her nymphomania in a cocoon of verbal respectability, she playfully chides Sloane for accusing her of seducing him and making her look cheap. Her bliss knows no bounds, as she informs Sloane that "Mamma is going to have a . . ." and then whispers, "A baby brother," in a farcical cross-conversation as she responds to a question from Kemp in the next room—"What are you having?" Her "A . . . bath, Dadda" is followed by her covering of her real situation with a diversionary bit: "You know that woman from the shops? . . . You wouldn't believe what a ridiculous spectacle she's making of herself" (*Plays*, 101).

When the possibility of Sloane's leaving Kath to live with Eddie arises, Kath threatens to go to the police about the murders. Sloane has already provided an explanation for Kemp's murder, and Eddie suggests a compromise by which each has Sloane for six months of the year. In a farcical blend of business and personal matters, Eddie prides himself on his arbitration skills acquired from the many business conferences in which he has been involved. Their pact agreed on, Kath requests of Eddie that Sloane be present at the birth of her child, for "it deepens the relationship if the father is there." In the kind of line he perfected with uninterrupted consistency in *Loot* and *What the Butler Saw*, Orton turns the clichés of everyday speech into his own epigrammatical irony in Eddie's response: "It's all any reasonable child can expect if the dad is present at the conception." Patting her cheek and bottom as is his wont upon leaving, he exhorts, "Be a good girl" (*Plays*, 149).

Sloane, a willing victim of seduction by Kath and Eddie, adapts himself easily to the convenience of others, thus ensuring his own comfortable place in their lives. He acquiesces passively to Kath's sexual advances, actively threatens Kemp in nightly visits to his room, uses Eddie's car for a night "on the razzle" with his own male friends, and avoids prison. He shares equally in both the creation of and solution to the problems of the family. He knows his charm has worked, not only with Kath but with Eddie, on whom his well-being depends. He feels sufficiently in power even to relate to Kemp the circumstances surrounding his murder of Kemp's employer:

It's like this see. One day I leave the Home. . . . They'd found me a likeable permanent situation. Canteen facilities. Fortnight's paid holiday. Overtime? Time and a half after midnight. A staff dance each year. What more could one wish to devote one's life to? I certainly loved that place. The air round Twickenham was like wine. . . . I thumbs a lift from a geyser who promises me a bed. . . . All you could wish he was, a photographer. He shows me one or two experimental studies. An experience for the retina and no mistake. He wanted to photo me. For certain interesting features I had that he wanted the exclusive right of preserving. You know how it is. I didn't refuse. . . . But then I got to thinking . . . and I gets up in the middle of the night looking for the film see. . . . Well it appears that he gets the wrong idea. Runs in. Gives a shout. And the long and the short of it is I loses my head which is a thing I never ought to a done with the worry of them photos an all. And I hits him. I hits him. (*Plays*, 125)

In what is both Sloane's fantasy of the good life and an honest confession about not intending to kill the photographer, Sloane reveals an innocence of nature that Orton has spoken of in his description of Sloane. His speech, however, does not change Kemp's mind about going to the authorities. In the ensuing physical struggle, Sloane, as in the earlier murder, does not intend to murder Kemp and is at first unaware that he has done so. His anger at Kemp changes to panic when he does realize what he has done, and once more his survival instinct takes over as he calls for help from Ed even as he pushes Kath away from the room. It is at this point that his entertainment of Kath stops and his entertaining of Eddie begins—his brief autobiographical monologue to Kemp being the transition from one to the other. The meaning of Orton's title—deriving from Kath's instruction to her father, to entertain Mr. Sloane—shifts variously in the course of the play. He is entertained by Kath in act 1, further entertained in act 2 as Kemp's death means Sloane's freedom, and, in a turnabout of entertaining, has bound himself to Kath and Eddie as their heterosexual and homosexual entertainer for the indefinite future. Like nature, he instinctively accommodates himself to whatever situation he is in. Orton's most sharply focused dramatization of his favorite theme—sexual sharing—Sloane is Orton's raisonneur for the decompartmentalization of sex and, as well, for the breaking of other artificial barriers erected by society.

Generally regarded as Orton's most autobiographical play, *Entertaining Mr. Sloane* not only draws on his mother and father in the characters of Kath and Kemp and on himself in Sloane, but also on the location of the Orton family home. The Orton home was situated near a canal into which industrial wastes were poured, so that Sloane's questioning of Kemp about why anyone would build a home in the midst of a rubbish dump is but another of the play's many autobiographical details.

His bisexual characterization of Sloane reflects his own ambiguity and the sense of his own sexual preference as a rational choice. Although from age 18 he lived a homosexual life, he, like Sloane, had had heterosexual interests during his Leicester years. In his *Diaries* he records at least one occasion even in his later life in which he responded briefly to a female on a street in Tangier and to another on a London bus. Orton also rejected what he regarded as the American stereotypical images of the homosexual as effeminate, and he was especially proud of his male physique. He worked hard at having the best-developed body among modern playwrights. Thus Sloane, in his initial meeting with Eddie, impresses him with a litany of the body-building athletic events in which he had participated.

Orton's father is briefly seen in the ineffectual Kemp and in the brief reference to his employment as gardener for the photographer murdered by Sloane. His mother, Elsie Norton, in a sketchy way, is reflected in details such as her meticulous attention to her appearance. When Sloane calls attention to Kath's repulsive toothlessness, she informs him that her dentures are in the kitchen in Stergene and that she hates people who are careless with their dentures. In her contest with Eddie for possession of Sloane, Kath clings to Sloane, only to be flung from him as her teeth fall to the floor. She crawls on the floor crying, "He's broke my teeth. Where are they?" A gruesomely farcical version of what is in *Entertaining Mr. Sloane* merely a humorously repulsive detail occurs in his next play, *Loot*, in the rolling of teeth from a corpse.

The un-Pinteresque naturalism that Orton fiercely claimed as his style is essentially invested in the liberties he takes with the hypocritical discrepancy between behavior and language, rather than in the shocking behavior and coarse details of the plays. Yet it is the latter on which negative criticism focused. But for opinions that mattered, the play was a success for the very reason that its discreditors panned it—its inventively fresh language. Labeled forever by Ronald Bryden as "the Oscar Wilde of welfare-state gentility," Orton has also been provided with linguistic labels whose local color can be appreciated only by the English. Eddie's reaction, for example, to Sloane's rough handling of Kath is to launch into a bit of sermonizing. Warning Sloane about "gratuitous violence," he bursts out, "Expensive equipment gone west now see? I'm annoyed with you, boy. Seriously annoyed. Giving us the benefit of your pauperism. Is this what we listen to the Week's Good Cause for? A lot of actors and actresses making appeals for cash gifts to raise hooligans who can't control themselves? I'd've given my check to the anti-Jewish League if I had known" (*Plays*, 146). His scolding of Sloane is but a hypocritical cover-up of his own attraction to Sloane and, at the same time, a warning to Sloane about future liberties the latter might take, either sexually or financially. The mixture of socially approved sentiments with societally rejected behaviors is an uncomfortable one, resulting in a lethal farce that left some critics and audiences unable to see beyond what they considered to be the vulgarity of the actions. In so doing, they failed to recognize the ironic elegance of Orton's wit that matches the vulgarity of his subject matter.

Critical reaction to *Entertaining Mr. Sloane* was predictable. Both extremes were plentiful, from the *Daily Telegraph*'s W. A. Darlington, who wrote about a feeling that "snakes had been writhing round my feet" to the *Evening Standard*'s John Mortimer (a contemporary dramatist), who approved: "And after what now seems a long time waiting round the moth-eaten wings of the commercial theatre something really quite good has come to me at last" (quoted in Lahr 1978, 167). Orton took special pride in what he considered the perceptive review of traditionalist and staid Harold Hobson of the *Sunday Times*, who saw *Entertaining Mr. Sloane* as a play that "begins as a joke about moral horror" and as such "goes on to develop a horror of its own." Describing it as a "*Northanger Abbey* of our contemporary stage," he judges it not as a "promising" work but "more like an end than a beginning" (quoted in Lahr 1978, 168). Alan Brien in the *Sunday Telegraph* caught the essence of the Ortonesque in calling attention to the

tone of voice of the actor [which] is disturbingly at variance with the words he speaks. For instance, when Peter Vaughan [as Eddie] looks at the sexy ruffian who has made his sister pregnant and murdered his father, and says with smiling menace: "Your youth pleads for leniency and, by God, I'm going to give it to you." Few non-English-speaking foreigners could grasp the deliberate incongruity of this simply by listening to the line literally translated and flatly spoken through an earphone. (Brien, n.p.)

Brien's point is a subtler distinction than Taylor's more general (and more obvious) one of the gap between the actions and the words. It is this nuanced incongruity that escaped critics like Darlington, who eventually did admit that his initial dislike of the play was actually a backhanded compliment. In his second viewing of the play, Darlington admitted to being "held throughout."

Orton received encouragement from an unlikely duo of dramatists— one a popular establishment dramatist who nonetheless found himself in some disrepute among the wave of new critics in the 1960s—Terence Rattigan—and the other the most avant-garde of the innovators of the new drama and a favorite of the new critics—Harold Pinter.

Rattigan, with his well-made plays for a fashionable middle-class audience, was by the late 1950s regarded by critic Kenneth Tynan as not only unfashionable but as the Formosa of the English stage. It was from Rattigan that Orton received his first fan letter. Acknowledging that his audience was "not likely to go and enjoy Joe's [plays]" (quoted in Lahr 1978, 170), he predicted that before the end of the decade Orton would write a masterpiece (169). In addition to admiring its classic construction, likening Orton to William Congreve, a dramatist Orton admired, Rattigan must have admired Orton's self-confidence in dealing directly with a subject, homosexuality, which he had had to disguise in heterosexual terms in his own plays. Of special delight to Orton was the censor's blue-penciling not the homosexual references in the play but the explic-it heterosexual material. Orton admitted to embarrassment at not being able to return Rattigan's "eulogies with any degree of conviction." Yet Rattigan extended his verbal encouragement with his contribution of £3,000 that made possible the transfer of *Entertaining Mr. Sloane* from the small Arts Theatre to the larger Wyndham's Theatre in the West End.

Pinter, like Rattigan, praised Orton's "instinctive grasp of construction." He referred to "an inner resonance of shifting references and at the same time a sustained sense of dramatic momentum from one sentence to the next" (Lahr 1978, 286). Although Pinter was the one living playwright whom Orton respected and although Pinter's influence is obvious in *The Ruffian on the Stair* and clearly toned down in *Entertaining Mr. Sloane*, Orton was reluctant to admit to Pinter's influence, noting, when questioned, other influences and pointing to the same Hollywood movies of the 1940s by which both writers had been shaped.

Most obvious in their stylistic differences, perhaps, is Orton's deliberately offensive treatment of sex as opposed to Pinter's subtextual handling—as, for example, in the contest over a glass of water between Ruth and Lenny in *The Homecoming* and in *The Birthday Party* in Meg Boles's giggling in an upstairs room when she brings Stanley's cocoa to him. There is no subtlety in Kath's calling attention to the fact that she is nude underneath her dress or her falling on her lodger at the end of act 1. Sex is nature's driving force in Orton's play, whereas in Pinter's it is part of a tissue of psychological power plays. Also unlike Pinter's characters who hide their identities in fear of knowing and being known, Orton's people expose and, if necessary, justify their intentions, taking care to do so in shibboleths. Even Sloane's two murders are comfortably accommodated in his pact with Eddie and Kath. Rewards or punishments are clearly not a consideration; rather, there is Orton's belief that "people are profoundly bad, but irresistibly funny."[3] Dramatizing the chaos of the moral order is the basis of Orton's naturalistic yet comic mayhem, described by Lahr as Orton's means of "disenchanting the credulous and of laughing the suffocating stereotypes off the stage."[4] Orton's deliciously shocking farcical stereotypes are a far cry from Pinter's hauntingly enigmatic reclusives.

In a conversation with an Egyptian journalist who was interested in translating Orton's *Loot* into Arabic and who saw "overwhelming" similarities between *The Homecoming* and *Entertaining Mr. Sloane*, Orton, ever

Lee Montague, George Turner, Sheila Hancock, and Dudley Sutton in *Entertaining Mr. Sloane*, Lyceum Theater, New York, 1965. *Courtesy of the Billy Rose Theater Collection at the New York Public Library for the Performing Arts, Astor, Lenox, and Tilden Foundations*

Malcolm McDowell and Beryl Reid in *Entertaining Mr. Sloane*, Royal Court Theatre, London, 1975. *Photograph by John Haynes*

Ronald Fraser and
Malcolm McDowell in
Entertaining Mr. Sloane,
Royal Court Theatre,
London, 1975.
*Photograph by John
Haynes*

Simon Ward and Kenneth
Cranham in *Loot,* London
Traverse Theatre Company at
the Jeanetta Cochran Theatre,
1966. *Photograph by John
Haynes*

Michael Bates and Sheila Ballantyne in *Loot,* London Traverse Theatre Company at the Jeanetta Cochran Theatre, 1966. *Photograph by John Haynes*

Sheila Ballantyne, Simon Ward, Kenneth Cranham, and Michael Bates in *Loot,* London Traverse Theatre Company at the Jeanetta Cochran Theatre, 1966. *Photograph by John Haynes*

Simon Ward, Sheila Ballantyne, Kenneth Cranham, and David Redmond in *Loot*,
London Traverse Theatre Company at the Jeanetta Cochran Theatre, 1966.
Photograph by John Haynes

Arthur O'Sullivan and Jill Bennett in *Loot*, Royal Court Theatre, London, 1975.
Photograph by John Haynes

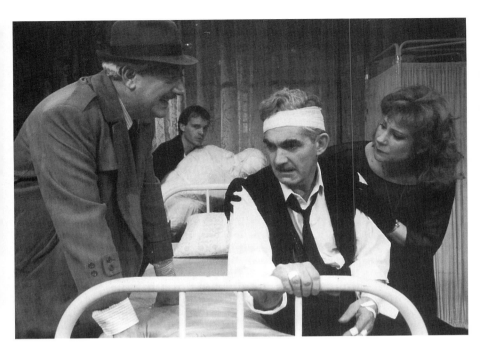

Joseph Maher, Zelko Ivanek, Charles Keating, and Zoe Wanamaker in *Loot*, Manhattan Theater Club, New York, 1986. *Photograph by Gerry Goldstein; courtesy of the Billy Rose Theater Collection at the New York Public Library for the Performing Arts, Astor, Lenox, and Tilden Foundations*

Zoe Wanamaker and Charles Keating in *Loot*, Manhattan Theater Club, New York, 1986. *Photograph by Gerry Goldstein; courtesy of the Billy Rose Theater Collection at the New York Public Library for the Performing Arts, Astor, Lenox, and Tilden Foundations*

Stanley Baxter, Ralph Richardson, and Coral Browne in *What the Butler Saw,* Queen's Theatre, 1969. *Photograph by Angus McBean, courtesy of the Angus McBean estate*

Betty Marsden and Kevin Lloyd in *What the Butler Saw,* Royal Court Theatre, 1975. *Photograph by David Montgomery*

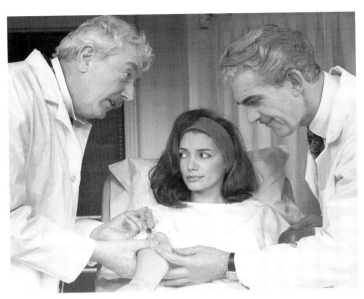

Joseph Maher, Carole Shelley, and Charles Keating in *What the Butler Saw,* Manhattan Theater Club, New York, 1989. *Photograph by Gerry Goldstein*

Bruce Norris, Patrick Tull, and Charles Keating in *What the Butler Saw,* Manhattan Theater Club, New York, 1989. *Photograph by Gerry Goldstein*

Michael Allinson and Terry Ashe-Croft in *The Good and Faithful Servant,* Actor's Playhouse, New York, 1988. *Photograph by Anita and Steve Shevett, courtesy of the Billy Rose Theater Collection at the New York Public Library for the Performing Arts, Astor, Lenox, and Tilden Foundations*

Laura Lane and William Carrigan in *The Good and Faithful Servant,* Actor's Playhouse, New York, 1988. *Photograph by Anita and Steve Shevett, courtesy of the Billy Rose Theater Collection at the New York Public Library for the Performing Arts, Astor, Lenox, and Tilden Foundations*

fierce about his originality, stated that the difference between him and
Pinter is that the latter would never share anyone sexually. Thus, unlike
Sloane, "*The Homecoming* doesn't spring from the way Harold [Pinter]
thinks" (*Diaries*, 238). In his diary entry of 11 July 1967 Orton records
that *The Homecoming*, produced nearly two years after *Entertaining Mr.
Sloane*, with its ending of shared sexual relationships, could not have
been written without *Entertaining Mr. Sloane* (*Diaries*, 238). In that play
Ruth, the wife of Eddie, refuses to return to America with her husband
and accedes to the arrangements by members of Eddie's family to stay in
London as a high-class prostitute, established in a flat by Eddie's family
for a high-class clientele such as Eddie's American academic colleagues
on their visits to England. The plays, in fact, end similarly. The last line
in Orton's play is Eddie's farewell to Kath. After the wrenching events,
he leaves her with "Well, it's been a pleasant morning. See you later." In
Pinter's play Ruth, after having made arrangements with his family on
her own terms, bids her husband farewell, "Don't become a stranger."

Taking a perverse delight in the moral condemnations of a W. A.
Darlington or an Emile Littler by responding to them with his own
pseudonymous critics, Orton was angered only by John Russell Taylor's
reference to him as a commercial playwright in Taylor's introduction to
the play published in Penguin's *New Dramatists 8*: "Living theatre needs
the good commercial dramatist as much as the original artist" (Lahr
1978, 171). Orton immediately shot off an angry note to his agent,
Peggy Ramsay, about using a West End appearance as something to be
sneered at "by people who judge artistic success by commercial failure"
(Lahr 1978, 171).

In New York the notices of *Entertaining Mr. Sloane* were mixed,
though Orton, during its previews, thought the production better than
that in London. The disapproval was loud and nearly unanimous, generally echoing the sentiments of Emile Littler, the English impressario
whose denunciation of the London production was the strongest of all.
Walter Kerr's opening statement in the *Herald-Tribune* that "*Entertaining
Mr. Sloane* is a bizarre black comedy which is simply not bizarre enough
to drive its black point home"[5] was bolstered by that of Howard
Taubman in the *New York Times* that "whether it is in earnest or not,
Entertaining Mr. Sloane is a singularly unattractive play."[6]

Orton's disappointment in the critical reception was only deepened
by his frustrating experience with American passport officials, who,
because of his prison record, would not grant him permission to stay in
New York as long as he wished.

John Tillinger—who directed *Entertaining Mr. Sloane* in a successful off-Broadway production 16 years later (1981) and highly successful productions of *Loot* and *What the Butler Saw* in the later 1980s at the Manhattan Theater Club—reinforced Orton's claim that Orton is an acquired taste. Americans, Tillinger claims, were not ready for Orton in the 1960s, but "after the appearance of such groups as Monty Python . . . [they] have acquired a taste for macabre wit and Orton's sense of anarchy."[7]

After its transfer to the West End, *Entertaining Mr. Sloane*, in a tie with William Naughton's *Alfie*, won an award as the best new English play, and Orton fell two votes short of Charles Wood as the most promising new playwright. The play was published immediately in Penguin's New English Dramatists series and as an August play-of-the-month in *Plays and Players*. It was sold to a Paris publisher in August 1964 and after that to publishers worldwide, as well as to film and television producers (the former not too successful)—all delighting Orton as the somebody that he had finally become.

Chapter Seven

Loot

"Is the world mad? Tell me it's not." This questioning of the world's sanity is posed by the recently widowed Mr. McLeavy, the only victimized innocent in Orton's play. He mouths every conceivable platitude with all the sincerity of the unthinking and is opposed by two authoritarian figures who offer their axiomatic wisdom with all the brilliant hypocrisy they can muster. In the end Mr. McLeavy becomes the only victim of the law and of the society embodied in that law.

Innocence of another kind belongs to McLeavy's son, Hal, and Hal's friend Dennis, petty thieves who live in a world in which honesty is a perversion, as in the case of Hal, whose only flaw in a thieving world is his inability to tell a lie. His compulsive truthfulness is brilliantly balanced by his anarchic insensitivity to feelings about his dead mother and by his role as abettor in the robbery of a bank next to the funeral parlor where his mother has been laid out.

Orton establishes his own world, with the Pinteresque plot-generating intruder no longer needed. In place of the comedy of manners of *Entertaining Mr. Sloane* there is a comedy of horrors, as Orton once described it. In this all-out attack on authority, Orton gives the plot away even before the play begins in an epigraph drawn from Bernard Shaw's *Misalliance*: "Anarchism is a game at which the Police beat you." What is at least equally scandalous, Lord Summerhays continues, is the British public's pretensions not to believe the accusation. Summerhays's contention is confirmed in Orton's Sergeant Truscott, who explains to McLeavy that loopholes in the law are sometimes used to solve crimes: "The process by which the police arrive at the solution to a mystery is, in itself, a mystery." McLeavy responds, "You've a duty to do. My personal freedom must be sacrificed" (*Plays*, 250–51). Using the law to satisfy his own greed, Truscott has no problem in recognizing that greed in others.

Orton's scathing farce, although aimed at victim and victimizer, is primarily invested in Truscott, a police officer operating under several aliases—inspector of the metropolitan water board and, as convenience dictates, of the post office. He has a soon-to-be worthy accomplice in

Nurse Fay, whom he accuses of causing Mrs. McLeavy's death, on the basis of her murders of seven previous husbands. She returns his charge with her own knowledge of the law: that she is innocent until proved guilty since that is the law. He is up to her poise: "You know nothing of the law. I know nothing of the law. That makes us equal in the sight of the law" (*Plays*, 254). Her insistence that the law is impartial meets with "Who's been filling your head with that rubbish?" (*Plays*, 254). He then threatens her with a forged confession, if that is necessary to secure her conviction.

Soon enough Fay will join Truscott in his exemplary undercover anarchism. Already bereaved of seven husbands—"one a year on average since I was sixteen. I'm extravagant, you see" (*Plays*, 202)—she is at the moment contemplating marriage with an eighth. Her currently projected victim is McLeavy. Her plans, however, are conveniently changed by a proposal from young Dennis, who is madly in love with her, and by her discovery of the loot now being hidden by Dennis and Hal. Like Hal, Dennis, and Truscott, she has only one need—money—and disguises that need in the pieties of her nursing profession and her Catholicism. When McLeavy informs her that a second marriage would be a physical impossibility, Fay, having already cast doubt on the genuineness of Mrs. McLeavy's practice of Catholicism, invokes the aid of the Fraternity of Little Sisters, whose Mother Mary Agnes treats McLeavy as a Catholic problem. McLeavy's response is that Mother Mary Agnes treats the washing of her feet as a Catholic problem and then, in one of Orton's subversive linguisms, questions whether Protestants have feet. Piously invoking religious sentiments, she reprimands him for the items atop his dressing table, "not only firearms but family planning equipment." She indicts his way of life as one for which "a Papal dispensation is needed to dust his room" (*Plays*, 197).

Orton's world is evocative of Thomas Middleton's from Orton's favorite century—the seventeenth. With Middleton, Orton shares a quality described by the editor of the 1640 posthumous edition of Middleton's plays: "Here is no bombast or fustian stuff, but every line weighed as with a balance, and every sentence placed with judgment and deliberation."[1] Orton balances not only line with line but crude line with equally crude physical details. Offendingly catching the audience off-guard is the essence of his humor. Hal exclaims, for example, "Bury her naked? My own Mum?" at the same time that he is considering what to do with her body, which he has just decoffined in order to make room for the money from his and Dennis's bank heist. Orton's balancing act does not shrink from physically repulsive dimensions, as in his attempts to hide or reinsert his mother's false teeth and the false eye that rolls on the floor during the frenzied attempts to hide the loot. Hal's compulsive honesty in a world whose authorities engage in lying as a way of life perversely balances his insensitivities.

Thus Orton joins Middleton in a lusty world in which anarchy is matched by the appearance of order, unreason with the appearance of logic, detachment with the appearance of sentiment, corruption and hypocrisy with the appearance of religion, criminality with the appearance of law enforcement, and, most important, lies (except for Hal) with the appearance of truth. The cancellation of one by the other is cause for Orton's celebration, as well as for the more traditional function of farce as exposure of the world's madness. The result is an anarchy controlled only by the order of Orton's artistry.

In a comic plot that suggests the actions of William Faulkner's *As I Lay Dying*, funeral arrangements are under way for the burial of Mrs. McLeavy. Hal, her son, and his friend Dennis are busily engaged in transferring the spoils of a bank robbery to the coffin and, for the moment, stuffing the corpse into a cupboard. Hal has no compunctions about the matter, although Dennis thinks that to remove the corpse is a shame, since the embalmers had done such a lovely job. The hasty solution to one problem only leads to the next. They are faced with the burial of the corpse, now out of the coffin, even as they think they have safely hidden their loot. They do not count on the intrusions of Fay, nurse to Mrs. McLeavy, who has her own plans for looting or Inspector Truscott of the Yard who, in the name of the law, practices legal anarchy. Consequently, a series of muddled attempts to safely bury the body and secure their money is complicated by their attempts to hide both from Fay and Truscott. The unemployed Hal has postburial dreams of going to a "smashing brothel," and Dennis is "on the wagon," "trying to get up sufficient head of steam to marry" (*Plays*, 209). When the action begins, Dennis has already been questioned by Truscott, who has been admitted into the house ostensibly as a water inspector. Calling the police office for protection, Dennis has been told that an officer was sent—that officer being none other than the Truscott who had beaten him once. Dennis's description of the attack suggests a lingering seventeenth-century linguism: "Gave me a rabbit punch. Winded me. Took me by the cobblers. Oh, strewth, it made me bad" (*Plays*, 210).

The stage is thus set for the manic actions that follow as their attempts to hide the money and to have the corpse buried are further complicated by problems such as the loosening of Mrs. McLeavy's false eye, which rolls downstage, only to reappear in a later scene. The ensuing series of dizzying confusions are linguistic as well as physical, as Hal's "mum," now a "mummy," is identified by Fay as her dressmaker's "dummy" in the trio's varied attempts to disguise their actions from Truscott.

Fast-paced complications continue in the reappearance of McLeavy, a bandaged victim of an accident involving the funeral cortege. He compounds the farcical scene by explaining that his bloodied condition is not the result of the crash but of the bites of a "fear-crazed Afghan hound that was being exercised at the time" (*Plays*, 238). When Hal and Dennis appear carrying the charred coffin still smoking from a fire caused by the accident, transfers of money and corpse involve a small casket in which, in keeping with traditional funeral practices, the vital organs of the dead are placed. A series of interrogations by Truscott ends in his arrest of Fay, who is eventually freed when McLeavy, instead, is charged with offensive remarks and threats to expose Truscott. The detective has now taken charge in the sharing of the spoils. He insists on safekeeping the casketful of money at the station. McLeavy's future is decided by the quartet of anarchists, and he is led to prison, where his accidental death will be arranged, and he will finally be buried with his wife. "That will be nice for him, won't it," Fay piously remarks. Both her comment and her tone echo the opening lines in the play, in which she refers to McLeavy's gift of a rose as a "nice thought" and to herself as a "nice person." It is no accident that Orton's revengeful fun begins and ends the play with the use of the emptiest and perhaps most frequently used adjective in the English language.

Anarchists, albeit not hypocrites, the two young hoodlums Hal and Dennis, the latter an employee of the funeral parlor handling arrangements for Mrs. McLeavy's burial, think nothing of violating either the law or traditional familial loyalties. Hiding the loot necessitates the moving around of the corpse, from which a false eye, a set of dentures, and a wedding ring are dislocated and roll on the floor. The two youths do, however, possess recognizably human qualities that set them apart from Truscott and Fay. Hal enjoys the kinds of fantasies many of Pinter's characters indulge in. His are of exotic trips and of running a "two-star brothel" that would eventually prosper into a "three-star brothel" in which there would be "birds" of a variety of colors and religions: "I'd have two Irish birds. A decent Catholic. And a Protestant. I'd make the Protestant take Catholics and the Catholic take Protestants." There would also be "a blonde bird who dyed her hair dark" (*Plays*, 226). Like Hal, Dennis also has a dream—his more realizable, perhaps, than Hal's. In love with Fay, he wants to marry her, marriage being one new experience he'd like to try. His hopes are raised when Fay, having lost McLeavy to the prison system, focuses on Dennis as her next marital prospect.

With greed and its accompanying hypocrisy the primary satirical targets of this the second of his full-length plays, Orton continues, as well, his attacks on sexual shibboleths, but these are woven in as a natural part of the larger aim. They come to life in the fantasies of Hal and Dennis about what their loot will buy. In his *Diaries* Orton has clearly stated that his two youthful roommates in *Loot* are homosexual but that he wants nothing "queer or camp or odd" about them. He rejects the "fag and drag" or the "Great American Queen" life-style and makes it plain that they must be played in "perfectly ordinary" style. In that ordinariness he includes Dennis's wanting to try the marriage experiment, another of Orton's many attempts to decompartmentalize and delabel sexual experience. So Hal dreams of running a brothel with exotic birds and Dennis wants to try marriage with a woman.

Finally, there is McLeavy, the one sincere upholder of the prevailing precepts of law, religion, medicine, and society in general. Like the father in *Entertaining Mr. Sloane*, McLeavy is a victim of the various anarchic schemes. Also like him, he is patterned after Orton's own father, whose gardening and special fondness for roses Orton treats as a farcical obsession in *Loot*. His concern over the flowers at the funeral reaches the level of the Jonsonian humors when, informed by Dennis that his "wreaths have been blown to buggery" in the funeral car smash-up, he suggests buying fresh ones: "Always some new expense" (*Plays*, 239). He also suggests that the revamped funeral services might appropriately include his photo of His Holiness, "only it's three Popes out of date" (*Plays*, 239).

Without relief, each character maneuvers his/her way in and around the events, according to the pressures of the moment, with varying degrees of detachments by all (except McLeavy) from their professed moral, ethical, religious, or emotional principles. The maneuvering includes attempts by Hal and Dennis to hide their loot, Fay's eighth attempt at marriage and money, McLeavy's need to see his wife properly buried, and, most dominant, Truscott's rampant use of legal authority to arrest someone regardless of guilt and to satisfy his own greed. He is a forerunner of Dr. Rance, the psychiatrist in *What the Butler Saw* who is obsessed with certifying everyone else in the play as insane.

However wild the actions of the play, it is the language in which
Orton embalms those actions that defines his style. In that language he
enjoys his revenge on the personal and professional outrages experienced for most of his life. In *Head to Toe*, Gombold prays for an ability
to rage correctly. Orton's ear for empty pieties, sloganeering, and
clichés seems at times to oversupply him with the means to so rage. His
brilliant subversions, sudden shifts, and distorted logic are the lethal
weapons aimed at societal taboos. When, for example, the mistreated
father-widower asks the inspector to produce a warrant or leave the
premises, the latter asks that his "cloth" be respected, whereupon the
victim asks, "Is he a priest?" The nurse responds, "If he is he's an
unfrocked one" (*Plays*, 247). A further shift follows immediately, when
the inspector identifies himself as Truscott, and the widower responds,
"What kind of name is that? Is it an anagram? . . . We're being made
the victim of some kind of interplanetary rag" (*Plays*, 248). In protest-
ing the inspector's intent to undress a seamstress's "dummy," which in
actuality is the corpse, one youth claims that "It isn't decent," and the
other says, "It's a Catholic." The inspector laughs mirthlessly, promising
that "the bobby won't interfere with it. He's a married man with children" (*Plays*, 249).

In a deconstruction of Holmesian myth, Truscott's deductive logic
demolishes any opponent with a fury that establishes him as a formida-
ble caricature of his famous prototype. With his lethal illogic and all the
authority of his position, he is able not only to garner 25 percent of the
take but to take the entire casket of loot into his possession for safekeeping. He brilliantly outmaneuvers Hal, Dennis, and Fay, at their own
game and is the prime mover of the play's action. His game, like that of
his victims, is money—the same greed at the heart of society in Ben
Jonson's *Everyman in His Humour* and Honoré de Balzac's *Human Comedy*.
Orton's mockery of greed leads, in John Russell Taylor's words, to "a
sublimely immoral, properly improper conclusion in which all, except
the unfortunate McLeavy, agree to share out the money and go on their
way" (Taylor, 133). Truscott's cool passion for money is surpassed only
by the agility with logic and language with which he disguises that
passion.

The result of his own prison experience, the irrational use of rational
investigative means by one corruptor against another is Orton's means
of raging correctly. To be rational in an irrational world is not, as one of
Orton's famous epigrams goes, rational. Along with parodies of
Holmes's famous deductive processes, Orton adds such other favorite

whodunit techniques as the cutting of phone lines and the command not to leave the premises without the inspector's permission.

In arriving on the scene, Truscott immediately displays his investigative prowess when, noticing the crucifix on Fay's breast, he concludes her background from the dent on one side and the engraving on the back, which reads, "St. Mary's Convent. Gentiles Only" (*Plays*, 214). He concludes that one of her quarrels with a previous husband had occurred at the Hermitage Private Hotel (a detail Orton refashions in *What the Butler Saw*), since in shaking her hand he noticed a roughness on one of her wedding rings. The roughness he associates with burns and salt, a gun and sea air, at a hotel "notorious for tragedies of this kind" (*Plays*, 214). Reciting a litany of the murder techniques she has used in disposing of her seven husbands, he makes it clear that his power over her supersedes hers over Hal and Dennis. He "finds it frightening that undeterred by past experience [she] is contemplating an eighth engagement" (*Plays*, 215). By elementary deduction, he identifies the dress she wears as Mrs. McLeavy's by its zip, "a type worn by elderly women." The accusation then suddenly veers to an interrogatory conclusion as he asks "When do you intend to propose to Mr. McLeavy?" (*Plays*, 215).

Truscott reinforces his verbal threats with crude physical force, balancing the terror of the action with the laughter of his dialogue as he does so. When Hal tells him the truth—that the money is in the coffin in the church—the skeptical Truscott accuses him of lying, knocks him to the floor, and shouts, "Under any other political system I'd have you on the floor in tears." Hal (crying) responds, "You've got me on the floor in tears" (*Plays*, 235). Insisting that the money was "In church! In church!," Hal is punched by Truscott until he screams with pain. The scene is interrupted only by the appearance of Fay with the bandaged McLeavy and news of the crash of the funeral procession.

Orton's use of Truscott to deconstruct the Holmesian myth is doubled in the person of Fay, who has her own detection process. No less a criminal than he, she has already established her territorial claims in the McLeavy household. Her disguise, like Truscott's, is her profession. When McLeavy presents her with a rose, a gesture she accepts as a "nice thought" for a "nice person," he notices his wife's shoes that Fay is wearing and adds that Mrs. McLeavy would not mind her having them. Later when she appears in his wife's black dress and is told by McLeavy that it suits her, she responds with a reference to "another piece of your wife's finery" and that "some people would censure me for wearing it" (*Plays*, 212). Her audacious pretense of innocence and of care for McLeavy's welfare has the same ring of authority as does Truscott's legal criminality. She convinces him early in the play of his need of someone to look after him, someone very much like herself: "You must marry again after a decent interval of mourning." When asked by McLeavy for an explanation of a decent interval, she assures him that "a fortnight would be long enough to indicate your grief. We must keep abreast of the times" (*Plays*, 197). In the same vein, at the end of the play, she bows her head to pray by the coffin, having suggested that the soon-to-be-murdered McLeavy be properly buried next to his wife. Her sentiments about McLeavy are matched by those of Hal, who, although much abused at the hands of Truscott, solemnly asserts the comforting thought that "the police can still be relied upon when we're in trouble" (*Plays*, 275). For the Edna Welthorpes in Orton's audiences, the comfort of the familiar axiom is wickedly satirized.

Fay's loyalties soon change from her wifelike concerns for McLeavy's welfare to motherly instincts toward Hal. She berates him for his "thieving from slot machines" and "deflowering the daughters of better men than yourself" (*Plays*, 199). Her concern, however, changes to suspicion when Hal refuses her the key to the cupboard where he and Dennis have hidden the corpse. Suspicions only grow as her own Holmesian interrogation easily worms the whole truth out of Hal, and she then joins the two youths in their maneuvers, having now gained the upper hand in the lives of McLeavy, Hal, and Dennis. In her struggle with Truscott— their scandalous audacity at times equal in its ferocious wit—he wins, warning her that he will invoke the authority of the "maxim of the force": never to search your own backyard, for "you may find what you are looking for" (*Plays*, 275).

Orton's attack on middle-class respectability takes as hilarious a turn in Fay's reshaping of social truisms as does Truscott's in his perversions of the legal process. To McLeavy, she explains away Hal's absence at his mother's funeral as an indication that Hal prefers to mourn in private. She, however, is "not in favour of private grief. Show your emotions in public or not at all" (*Plays*, 198).

Similarly, Hal and Dennis are mouthpieces for Orton's farcical jests about sexual compartmentalism. When Hal confronts Dennis with the fact that Fay is so much older, Dennis remembers his dad's advice that "an experienced woman is the finest thing that can happen to a lad." Hal, who, it is suggested, may have also bedded Fay, calls attention to her being "three parts Papal nuncio. She'd only do it at set times" (*Plays*, 210).

Some of Orton's most biting wit comes at the expense of McLeavy, the befuddled innocent in the farce. When, for example, he announces that he has ordered 400 rose trees to be planted a stone's throw from the church, as Mary McLeavy's Memorial Rose Garden, its beauty, he says, would put paradise to shame. Fay asks whether he has ever seen paradise, and he responds, "Only in photographs." "Who took them?" she asks. He answers, "Father Jellicoe. He's a widely travelled man" (*Plays*, 217).

Leaps of logic exist in abundance, primarily in Truscott's ratiocinative lines. In an incident that suggests the famous doorbell incident in Ionesco's *Bald Soprano*, the sleuth, having just ridden roughshod over personal liberties, excuses Fay to answer the ringing doorbell, reminding her that such a liberty is "how we tell whether or not we live in a free country" (*Plays*, 235). The incident contains the same annihilative mechanicalness on which Ionesco built his absurdist plays.

Loot, thus, is one long, nonstop series of wittily contradictory lines and images that defy all logic and reality yet are pronounced with an authority that carries the convincing ring of logic. The emptiness of the words balanced by their unremittingly forceful delivery is Orton's celebration of anarchy. If this deadly balance is not realized in a production, inevitable failure is the consequence, as demonstrated in the first production of *Loot* in a pre-London run (1965) and in New York (1968). In later productions in London in (1966) and New York (1986), the balance was successfully realized and Orton's reputation firmly established.

Orton's own reaction even to the first successful London production was not wholehearted: "Ideally, it should be nearer *The Homecoming* than *I Love Lucy*. . . . I think it's very funny. But it's aimed purely at making an audience laugh. And that isn't the prime aim of *Loot*" (*Plays*, 21). In response to the charge of the play's offensiveness, Orton contended that "if you're absolutely practical—and I hope I am—a coffin is a box. One calls it a coffin and once you've called it a coffin it immediately has all sorts of associations" (quoted in Gordon, 95). To an outraged audience Orton identifies the box as reality and, in his oft-quoted line, points out that "reality is the ultimate outrage" (*Plays*, 21), as are false teeth and eye.

In his review of another successful production of *Loot* at the Royal Court Theatre in 1975, Irving Wardle described the play as "a cold-blooded masterpiece; it is at once a glorious parody of the detective thriller, a goldmine of comic disassociations of language, and a piece that comes to mind whenever the police get trapped on the wrong side of the law."[2]

The reviews of the 1986 production in New York were nothing if not raves. Mel Gussow lauded *Loot* as "a priceless contemporary example . . . [of the author's] attack on the audience's collective funnybone" and attributed its success to "Mr. Tillinger [director] and his fine company of farceurs [who] keep cool heads and reflexes as quick as those of a racing horse."[3] Frank Rich described the play as "timeless because its author's rage against hypocrisy is conveyed not by preaching or idle wisecracks but by the outrageous farcical conception and by pungent, stylized dialogue in the tradition of Wilde and Shaw." Twenty years after its initial success, it had "lost none of its furious wit or capacity to shock."[4]

Loot invites a variety of critical approaches. One of these—advanced by Maurice Charney and Lahr—is the placing of Orton's farce in the oldest classical traditions far beyond those of contemporary farceurs like Wilde or Feydeau. Orton's farcical sense is essentially that of nature in rebellion against restriction. It is, for example, the nature of Hal to steal, to subvert sexual convention, and, in what is his peculiar perversity, to respond to Dennis's "Why can't you lie like a normal man?" with "I can't, baby. It's against my nature" (*Plays*, 207). In his incisive chapter on *Loot* as quotidian farce, Charney regards the crudeness and vulgarity of language and image as a return "to its roots in Plautus and the Italic fertility and harvest rituals that farce celebrates" (Charney, 82). The classical farces themselves, he asserts, are "closer to black comedy than to the upper-class comedy-of-manners assumptions of Restoration comedy . . . or even the middle-class gentility that Feydeau so deftly titillated in his brilliant social comedies" (Charney, 82).

Lahr, too, calls attention to Orton's roots in classical farce, which dealt with adultery rather than, as in the French farces and those of Ben Travers, with the idea of adultery, "which turned out to be innocuous, after all" (Lahr 1978, 187). What is missing in the Parisian boulevard farces, the English Whitehall farces, and the "well-plotted Ben Travers escapades" is the closeness to tragedy brought about by the "healthy shock . . . at those moments when an audience *stops* laughing" (Lahr 1978, 187). It is this point at which laughter stops that vestiges of Pinter remain. Pinter's audiences may laugh, albeit with some discomfiture or embarrassment, throughout his lines. Orton's hilarity is so broad that audiences do not realize its horror until that moment when shock replaces laughter.

In one of the earlier scholarly views of the play, John Russell Taylor wrote of *Loot* as a conventional thriller that works on the level of parody—"as a play about plays and play conventions rather than . . . about life" (Taylor, 132). He found it less satisfactory than *Entertaining Mr. Sloane*, whose comedy-of-manners style Taylor prefers to the slight "shift in the direction of farce" (Taylor, 131) and the tendency toward abstraction in *Loot*. Taylor ignores the growing detachment in Orton's style, with its roots in anarchic nature, whose own laws are an instinctual protest against the restrictions of imposed authority.

Katharine Worth sees Orton's ability to shock and offend as his arresting originality—the result of a detachment that, although not fully realized until *What the Butler Saw*, is still a "cool convention" that pushes "the dark elements so much to the fore without losing the sense of health." Orton's is a "dream subversiveness sometimes taken by critics firmly towards social commentary, a spur to social conscience, rather than, as one might have thought, a diabolical holiday from it."[5]

Perhaps nowhere is Orton's view of rebellious nature more evident than in frequent routine newspaper accounts of crimes—accounts that support one of the lines in his plays that all classes are criminal and therefore farcical. One such account is a brief article in the *New York Times* about a $2 million recovery of a Brink's armored truck theft of $5.4 million. The suspects charged with receiving or possessing the stolen money include Rev. Patrick M. J. Maloney, a 61-year-old Melkite priest; Samuel J. Millar, a convicted IRA smuggler; and Thomas F. O'Connor, a retired Rochester police officer. There was no evidence that any of the loot found its way to the IRA. The mixture of legal and religious authorities might well be the basis for an Ortonesque plot.[6]

Orton's targets include victims as well as their corruptors. In England, as one of the characters in *Loot* explains, "respect for the law is proverbial," so that, C. W. E. Bigsby writes, "people would willingly give power to arrest to the traffic lights if three women magistrates and a Liberal MP would only suggest it." Orton's "plot is, indeed, a neat reversal of the standard mystery play, a parody of that restoration of order which is inherent in the detective story and the well-made realistic play alike."[7] Orton reversed the "restoration" ending of traditional plays and in doing so "relied on his audience's failure to recognize the parodic thrust and took pleasure in their discomfiture" (Bigsby, 35). It is like the pleasure Orton took in furtive observations of library users reacting to his book defacings.

Among the many general comparisons of Orton with Wilde, John
Simon points out a particular scene in *Loot* that he regards as an example
of a disciple's digesting of a lesson from a master.[8] He draws parallels
between Lady Bracknell's examination of Jack as a possible husband for
Gwendolyn and Fay's interrogation of Hal about Dennis as a possible
husband:

L.B.:   . . . Do you smoke?

JACK: Well, yes, I must admit I smoke.

L.B.:   I am glad to hear it. A man should always have an
            occupation of some kind. . . . How old are you?

JACK: Twenty-nine.

L.B.:   A very good age to be married at. I have always
            been of opinion that a man who desires to get mar-
            ried should know either everything or nothing.
            Which do you know?

JACK: (*after some hesitation*) I know nothing, Lady
            Bracknell.

L.B.:   I am pleased to hear it. I do not approve of any-
            thing that tampers with natural ignorance.[9]

Orton is no less witty in his low-life parody of Wilde. As Simon
points out, his use of hesitation in Nurse Fay's advice to Hal is an
appropriate parallel to Lady Bracknell's recommendation of ignorance
to Jack:

FAY: Have you known him long?

HAL: We shared the same cradle.

FAY: Was that economy or malpractice?

HAL: We were too young then to practice, and economics
            still defeat us. . . .

FAY: . . . You will be forced to associate with young men
            like yourself. Does that prospect please you?

HAL: I'm not sure.

FAY: Well, hesitation is something to be going on with.
            We can build on that. What will you do when
            you're old?

HAL:	I shall die.
FAY:	I see you're determined to run the gamut of all experience. That can bring you nothing but unhappiness. (*Plays*, 200)

Simon concludes his review of the 1986 New York production of *Loot* with his assertion that Fay's interrogation "may be merely funny when read; well acted on stage, it is a bloody riot" (Simon, 135).

Among those likening Orton to Wilde is Rattigan, who adds the caveat that Orton goes even beyond Wilde in the bite of his aphoristic wit. The bite referred to by Rattigan has an ironic parallel in Orton's physical comparison of himself with Wilde, this from an author who proudly proclaimed himself the most physically fit of modern playwrights: "I didn't suffer the way Oscar Wilde suffered from being in prison. But then Wilde was flabby and self-indulgent" (*Diaries*, 15).

The Wildean influence on Orton, however, is most clearly seen in the plot of his last play, *What the Butler Saw*, in which the lessons learned at a master's feet are undeniably present.

There is an interesting literary lineage among four famous modern dramatists who were homosexual—Wilde, Coward, Rattigan, and Orton. Wilde and Coward wrote popular comedies of manners about middle-class society without endangering their reputations by writing overtly about homosexual matters. Similarly, Rattigan wrote plays of solidly middle-class society but disguised homosexuality in heterosexual relationships—the most notable of these being *Separate Tables* and *Variation on a Theme*. Orton's direct treatment of sexuality, whatever its nature, runs the gamut of all shades of sexual experience: heterosexuality, homosexuality, bisexuality, hermaphroditism, and, in his last play, transvestism and incest. Decompartmentalized, they are Orton's force of nature in rebellion against institutionalized attitudes. In Orton's world marriage, especially, excuses no one the freaks' roll call.

As the madness in *Loot* turns the known world topsy-turvy, however, sexuality, one part of that world, functions in a minor way, mostly in the fantasies of the two youths who wish to use the loot to realize their fantasies—of brothels in one case and the marriage experiment in the other. Sex has little or no part in the experiences of Fay and Truscott and is absorbed entirely in their greed. In the end, *Loot*, although a satire on hypocrisy and greed, is a festive farce, subversive in the undermining of established authorities and marvelous in the metamorphosis of low-life actions and aphoristic speech into scandalous entertainment that contrasts sharply with that of the campers in *The Erpingham Camp*.

The 1986 production at the Manhattan Theater Club was hilarious enough to put some of the audience on the floor in tears and shocking enough for others to leave with offended sensibilities. Such audience responses would have delighted Orton had he lived to see them and possibly inspired his shooting off of a few letters from Mrs. Edna Welthorpe and Donald H. Hartley.

In the freakishness that only the Ortonesque natural rhythms of life can anticipate, *Loot*, after being victimized by unsuccessful productions in England and the United States two decades earlier, became victimizer for one of its actors, Leonard Rossiter. A master of farce acting, Rossiter collapsed in a highly acclaimed revival of the play in 1984. The irony doubles in the parallel of the real-life incident with the subject of the play. A tripling of the irony is Orton's original title of the play, *Funeral Games*, a title replaced by *Loot* at the suggestion of Halliwell. Anthony Masters reviewed the strength of the production as the "fastest performance I can remember . . . [in its] maintaining of a farcical pace while squeezing the last drop of laughter from the outrageous dialogue. Some time, Mr. Lynn [director] must have a shot at Ben Jonson, where that balance is most necessary yet hardest to strike."[10] As with the irony of the opening of the posthumous production of *What the Butler Saw* at one of London's most famous commercial theaters, Orton would have enjoyed the many-leveled irony of this production of *Loot*, not the least of which is the implied comparison of himself with Jonson.

Chapter Eight
What the Butler Saw

RANCE:	. . . I've published a monograph on the subject [madness]. I wrote it at the university. On the advice of my tutor. A remarkable man. Having failed to achieve madness himself he took to teaching it to others.
PRENTICE:	And were you his prize pupil?
RANCE:	There were some more able than I.
PRENTICE:	Where are they now?
RANCE:	In mental institutions.
PRENTICE:	Running them?
RANCE:	For the most part. (*Plays*, 386)

Had Orton lived to see the first production of *What the Butler Saw*, he might have celebrated a kind of madness in the ironies associated with the posthumous production. The play opened at the Queen's Theatre in the heart of the West End on 5 March 1969, with a cast of stars led by Sir Ralph Richardson in the role of an inspector of mental hospitals, Dr. Rance. Before his death, Orton, in a conversation with a producer, had spoken of the wonderful joke it would be to have his play produced in the "Theater of Perfection" as he dubbed the Haymarket Theatre—to him the home of the kind of middle-class entertainment enjoyed by his epistolary alias, Mrs. Edna Welthorpe. The play was indeed produced at a commercial theater. Further irony resides in the all-star cast, despite which the production failed and about which Orton had opined to the producer that, although he admired Richardson, he had doubts about his comic talent. The production proved Orton right.

In her review of the production, Hilary Spurling called attention to the discrepancy between two "implacably opposed" styles, the "old and new in violent combat"[1]—one designed never to give offence (the management of Tenants) and the other whose very existence depends on offending audience sensibilities. The clash of styles, Spurling continues, is most glaring in the performance of Richardson, who spoke his lines with "extraordinary chanting, as though the text had been delivered to him in the form of church responses" (Spurling, 344). Another ironic touch is the abolition of the theater censorship law in 1968, prior to the production but after the death of Orton. A pattern of censoring had set in with earlier plays. During the successful production of *Loot* in 1965, Orton had particularly enjoyed talking about the censor's objection to heterosexual references while completely ignoring the "homosexual bits" (Bigsby, 48, 49). The Lord Chamberlain had also cut offensive language in *The Erpingham Camp* for its airing on television. With the passage of censorship abolition there was no official threat, but in its place came one imposed by Richardson, who insisted on the use of a cigar rather than a phallus in a big scene at the play's end.

The name of Richardson continues into yet another irony: a history of first production failures of Orton's plays. Without the financial aid provided by Rattigan, *Entertaining Mr. Sloane* may not have made the transfer from the small Arts Theatre to a money-making larger West End theater. Like the first production of *Loot* (which failed in its provincial tour), *What the Butler Saw* (1969) failed because of misjudgments in both casting and directing. One lonely voice of approval was that of Frank Marcus, who commented that the farce "will live to be accepted as a comedy classic of English literature."[2] Not until 1975, when the Royal Court put on an Orton retrospective, and 1986, when the Manhattan Theater Club mounted a successful production, was Marcus's prophecy realized.

The play, agreed on generally by critics and scholars as Orton's best, is yet another parody, both in its subject matter and style. Having dealt with the hypocrisy of sexual taboos in *Entertaining Mr. Sloane*, the corruption of law enforcement in *Loot*, institutionalized entertainment in *The Erpingham Camp*, corporate paternalism in *The Good and Faithful Servant*, and religion in *Funeral Games*, Orton aimed his most devastating and hilarious wit at the new religion—psychiatry—in *What the Butler Saw*.

Literary genres are also a target of Orton's farce. Having parodied the comedy of manners in *Entertaining Mr. Sloane* and the mystery genre in *Loot*, he now turned to farce, particularly one of the oldest of farce premises—twins separated at birth who must eventually reunite with each other and their families. The single most necessary convention in this process is the disguise—one that Orton carries to dizzyingly confusing heights. The multiplicity of Orton's disguises results in the expected confusions of names and identities, teeter-totter plot complications caused by a fast-paced series of exits and entrances, the big scene, and the deus ex machina ending. The sheer multiplication of each of the plot conventions is unprecedented and gives Orton opportunity to demonstrate his subversive and witty anarchy as in no other of his farces.

In *Loot*, for example, disguises exist in the roles characters assume, such as Inspector Truscott's claim to be an inspector from the water board. Nurse Fay, as well, disguises her actions in the pieties of her Catholic religion. In both characters the disguises exist to personify institutional corruption. In *What the Butler Saw*, the disguises are physical—clothes—and they exist from the very start to propel manic actions. They propel not only Orton's satire on the corruption of authority figures but his wider inquiry into the philosophical nature of reality. The physical actions, thus, take the play far beyond the satirical thrusts of his earlier plays to metaphysical questions of identity and of man's attempts to hold in check forces of nature that call those attempts into question.

The action begins innocently enough in a mental institution in which the director, Dr. Prentice, with an irresistible proclivity for attractive secretaries, interviews an applicant, Geraldine Barclay. In answer to his questions, she can produce no father or mother, except for one important bit of biographical information: that her mother had been a chambermaid at the Station Hotel. Her stepmother, she further explains, died in an explosion in which a statue of Sir Winston Churchill was damaged, a part of which (a phallus-cum-cigar), became imbedded in her stepmother. A box that Geraldine carries contains that part and becomes the detail with which Orton in his conclusion draws together the loose ends of the play. Prentice's interview of Geraldine, whose sorry qualifications include her ability to take dictation at only 20 words a minute and her lack of mastery of the typewriter keyboard, then moves to its next stage, Prentice's request that she undergo a physical examination. Despite her request for the presence of another woman, he issues his first order to her: "Undress." It is an order that he will issue repeatedly, to Nicholas Beckett and Sergeant Match, as well as to Geraldine. In succession, he orders one pair of dressing and undressing in order to solve a problem created with the previous one.

Disguises, like the masks in Greek plays, become the order of the day, beginning with the unexpected appearance of Mrs. Prentice, from whom Prentice must hide Geraldine. His wife, nymphomaniacal in her search for sexual satisfaction, has just returned from a meeting of a lesbian club and from a night at the Station Hotel. She is followed by a hotel page,

Nicholas Beckett (with whom she had spent the night), who brings with him incriminating photographs taken by the hotel manager. To Nick's comment that options on the photographs had been given to a prospective buyer, she responds with Ortonesque aplomb and wit: "When I gave myself to you the contract didn't include cinematic rights" (*Plays*, 370). Financially bereft, Nick intends to blackmail her with a request for money and for the position of secretary to Dr. Prentice, the position for which Geraldine is in the process of being interviewed. In approaching her husband about the hiring of Nick, Mrs. Prentice explains Nick's resorting to rape as the result of depression "by his failures in commerce." She then informs Geraldine that the position is no longer open.

Her intrusion on her husband's attempted affair with Geraldine forces him to begins a dazzling series of disguises and counter-disguises, the first of which involves his hiding the clothes of Geraldine, now nude behind a screen. He finds a convenient flower vase which becomes the focus of subsequent complications. In compliance with his wife's request that he hire Nick, he soon has Nick in shorts and Geraldine in Nick's uniform. Changes of dress increase at a frantic pace as one disguise only breeds the necessity for another. Even his wife, who arrives from her hotel escapade naked under her coat, must be accommodated, the only available dress being Geraldine's. A box Nick carries contains Mrs. Prentice's costume—a wig and a leopard-spotted dress—her disguise during her visit to the Station Hotel and one that Sergeant Match will appropriately don at the conclusion of the play. Thus the clothes of Geraldine, Nick, Match, and Mrs. Prentice become the modus operandi of Orton's plot complications.

Orton parodies another of farce's oldest conventions—the doubling of a character, situation, or object. Orton uses the box Geraldine brings with her, with its contents of the missing part of Sir Winston Churchill's statue, as a plot device to begin and end the play, and he uses Nick's box, containing Mrs. Prentice's attire, as a complicating factor in that plot device. Orton begins his complications with the contents of Nick's box and concludes with that in Geraldine's. It is not enough to have one sexually mad psychiatrist, Prentice; there must be the greedy and theory-obsessed practitioner, Rance, who detects in every action a confirmation of one of his theories. There is a set of twins and not two but three detectivelike interrogators—Prentice, Rance, and the police officer, Match.

Unexpected entrances and exits, another necessary farce convention, continually create new problems for Prentice, until at one point Mrs.

Prentice utters, "Doctor, doctor! The world is full of naked men running in all directions" (*Plays*, 437). When Geraldine appears in a new disguise and Nick suggests restoring normality by one more change of clothes, Prentice replies that he would have to account for the secretary and page boy (the false identities of the two young people). Reminded by Geraldine that the disguises are only disguises and that, therefore, the newly created identities do not exist, Prentice offers one of Orton's many entertaining contortions of logic: "When people who don't exist disappear the account of their departure must be convincing" (*Plays*, 419). The real madness of Prentice's circular logic, expressed in self-defense, carries its own practical function for him, even as it plays havoc with the various identities that keep changing despite his attempts to stabilize them. The changing relationship of fantasy to reality becomes a precarious balancing act as manic actions and psychiatric insanity keep pace with each other, one illusion replacing another with eye-dazzling speed.

Without any evidence except his own dogmatic beliefs, the theory-spouting Rance imposes his double-incest interpretation on the events, only, in a freakish turnabout, to have his fantasy subsequently proved to be a reality. Thus the appropriateness of the epigraph to the play—a quotation from Cyril Tourneur's *The Revenger's Tragedy*: "Surely we're all mad people, and they / Whom we think are, are not."

In a perceptive essay Katharine Worth writes of Orton's view of life as a dream turned into a nightmare, where "ideas keep turning into their opposites on his stage. It's always the clergyman who is the lecherous killer, the policeman—who starts off seeming a solid Dr. Watson figure . . . who turns out to be the most adept in corruption" (Worth, 76). In this black farce two psychologists rival each other in madness—one sexually and the other professionally—in much the same manner as the two clerics in *Funeral Games* vie for the title of chief corruptor. With psychiatry replacing religion as a source of hypocrisy in the twentieth century, Dr. Rance, inspector of mental institutions, is the maddest of all. Prentice, like the earlier McCorquodale, merely attempts to survive his initial disaster—attempts that force him to tell lies that necessitate disguises.

To Geraldine's questioning of the necessity of a physical examination for a secretarial applicant, Prentice replies that he needs to see the effect of her stepmother's death on her legs. He then reports the "febrile condition of her calves" as justification for the examination and gains her sympathy by a description of his wife's nymphomania and the resulting malice he has had to endure. She offers to cheer him up, and he, in turn, promises that she can test his new contraceptive device. To all of which she replies that she would be "delighted to help you in any way I can, doctor" (*Plays*, 368). Her off-setting innocent acquiescence is Orton's comic means of devictimizing her, thus detaching the audience emotionally, an Ortonesque hallmark rendered so effectively in the famous thrashing of Hal by Truscott in *Loot*.

This balancing act permeates the farce, with Orton's epigrammatic genius reaching such heights as in Mrs. Prentice's use of cultural clichés to justify her otherwise socially unjustifiable behavior. Like her husband who later fends off an accusation with the plea that he is a married man, Mrs. Prentice, upset at the photographs taken by the hotel manager, pleads with him, "Oh, this is scandalous. I am a married woman" (*Plays*, 370). When she notices her husband's attempt to hide Geraldine's dress, she accuses him of transvestism, in one of Orton's lethally witty attacks on contemporary mores: "I'd no idea our marriage teetered on the edge of fashion." To which, with an equally devastating freshening-up of a cliché—in this case a biblical one—Prentice responds, "Our marriage is like the peace of God—it passeth all understanding" (*Plays*, 373). Orton's epigrammatic wit is at its best in this exposure of the disjunction between language and behavior.

In yet another balancing act of style and substance, Orton pits a technical staple of farce—doors—against psychiatric insanity. Doors are especially prominent in popular Feydeau farces that Orton attended in London. He uses the farce convention here to parody itself, and, as well, to satirize psychiatric madness. When Dr. Rance, as inspector of mental institutions, appears, he is immediately suspicious of the many doors in the consulting office: "Was this house designed by a lunatic?" Pouring another whiskey, Prentice replies, "Yes, we have him here as a patient from time to time" (*Plays*, 377).

Questioning further the architectural features, Rance asks if the skylight is functional, and Prentice replies, "No. It's perfectly useless for anything—except to let light in" (*Plays*, 377). The nature of Rance's investigative techniques is apparent from the start. Every detail he observes must have some significance other than the obviously pragmatic one. Each significance then only leads to another, with one becoming more ludicrous than its predecessor.

The architectural details are soon lost in the flurry of Rance's next observation—this one more susceptible to psychiatric significance: the nude Geraldine, who Prentice, to cover up his intended indiscretion, claims is a patient. On the basis of Prentice's fabrication of her background, Rance decides immediately that she must be certified. She is the first victim in a series of Rance's instant certifications or attempted certifications. His psychiatric diagnoses of those he meets run a parallel line with the physical disguises Prentice finds himself forced to impose on others. Thus, Geraldine, Nick, and Match are doubly victimized—their identity confusions resolved only in the final disclosure scenes.

In another farcical doubling, Geraldine, having already been subjected to questioning by Prentice, undergoes interrogation by Rance. Passionately imposing his theories on her answers to his questions, he proclaims her denial of rape by her father as an automatic "yes," for that is only "elementary feminine psychology." He claims her as a textbook case: "A man beyond innocence, a girl aching for experience. He finds it difficult to reconcile his guilty secret with his spiritual convictions. . . . She seeks advice from her priest. The Church, true to her ancient traditions, counsels chastity. The result—Madness" (*Plays*, 383).

Rance has now set in motion what turns out to be a landslide of psychological clichés, turning every word he hears and every action he witnesses into a case study of his theories. When Rance exits, Prentice turns his attention to Nick in the hope of acquiring clothes for Geraldine, and the merry-go-round of costume changes commences in earnest. Ordering Nick to take off his uniform, however, only fuels his wife's accusations of transvestism. Naturalism serves Orton's parodic style, as the consulting-room screen of the doctor doubles as the requisite screen behind which disguises are shed and acquired in the standard farce.

The frenzy of complications begun with the unexpected arrivals—first of Mrs. Prentice, Nick, and then Rance—is quadrupled by that of Sergeant Match, who is there to inquire about Nick and about the missing parts of Sir Winston Churchill's statue. As the object of a possible lawsuit by the Council, with the support of the Conservative and Unionist Party, those parts are the subject of his interrogation of Nick, dressed as Geraldine. In parodic investigative jargon, he asks "her" to "produce or cause to be produced" the missing part. Not missing a beat, Orton blends the formality of investigative language with sexual inuendos in Match's reply:

NICK: What do they look like?

MATCH: You're claiming ignorance of the shape and structure of the objects sought?

NICK: I'm in the dark.

MATCH: You handled them only at night? We shall draw our
          own conclusions.

NICK: I'm not the kind of girl to be mixed-up in that kind
          of thing. I'm an ex-member of the Brownies. (*Plays*,
          405)

Ordering yet another of the many medical examinations in the farce,
he appoints Mrs. Prentice to examine her (him), since "only women are
permitted to examine female suspects" (*Plays*, 406). Then, as Geraldine
enters, dressed as Nick, the first act ends with Match's command: "I
want a word with you, my lad" (*Plays*, 407). Geraldine is now Nick, and
Nick is Geraldine. Confusions multiply furiously from this point on,
until even the keenest in an Orton audience finds himself, at moments,
questioning who is who.

The second act begins with Match shaking his head as Geraldine,
dressed as Nick, attempts to correct his confusion with a true account of
things. Like Hal in *Loot*, "he" is straightforward, but Match is only baffled by the truth. To Prentice he asserts, "This is a boy, sir. Not a Girl. If
you're baffled by the difference it might be as well to approach both
with caution." Prentice claims that the charge by Geraldine-dressed-as-
Nick about Prentice's strange behavior is ridiculous. Claiming "I'm a
married man," he leads Match into one of Orton's most choice epigrams:
"Marriage excuses no one the freaks' roll-call" (*Plays*, 409). Like the
Prentices earlier, Match freely offers his sentiments on marriage as a justification for his theories. "Nick's" truthful confession of her real sex,
however, does not convince Match and only builds his suspicion of
Prentice as pervert and madman. Match then orders yet a third examination of Geraldine.

Match follows one witty dictum with another when Prentice, faced
with the likelihood of being charged with homosexuality, claims he is a
heterosexual. Match responds, "I wish you wouldn't use these
Chaucerian words. It's most confusing" (*Plays*, 411).

Orton's real madman in the play, however, is Rance, who turns his psychiatric gaze on Prentice and challenges him to prove the charge of
molesting Match by committing the act. To vindicate himself, Prentice
orders Match to undress, and Match finds himself being examined, taking
medication, and eventually donning Mrs. Prentice's leopard-spotted dress.

Rance reaches psychiatric apotheosis in his conclusions about the
events he has witnessed. Having proved, Holmesian style, that Prentice
has done away with his secretary, Rance now anticipates literary success
as a best-seller writer of melodrama:

Lunatics are melodramatic. The subtleties of drama are wasted on them. The ugly shadow of anti-Christ stalks this house. Having discovered her Father/Lover in Dr. Prentice the patient replaces him in a psychological reshuffle by that archetypal figure—the devil himself. Everything is now clear. The final chapters of my book are knitting together: incest, buggery, outrageous women and strange love—cults craving for depraved appetites. All the fashionable bric-a-brac. A beautiful but neurotic girl has influenced the doctor to sacrifice a white virgin to propitiate the dark gods of unreason. (*Plays*, 427)

Carried away by his fantasy, Rance interrupts himself to inject an actual line of purple prose from his proposed novel: "When they broke into the evil-smelling den they found her poor body bleeding beneath the obscene and half-erect phallus" (*Plays*, 427). He concludes his monologue with a self-serving commentary on the great social rewards of his investigation:

My unbiased account of the infamous sex-killer Prentice will undoubtedly add a great deal to our understanding of such creatures. Society must be made aware of the growing menace of pornography. The whole treacherous avant-garde movement will be exposed for what it is—an instrument for inciting decent citizens to commit bizarre crimes against humanity and the state. . . . You have under your roof, my dear, one of the most remarkable lunatics of all time. We must institute a search for the corpse. (*Plays*, 427–28)

Rance's quackery is total as he pronounces Prentice "a transvestite, fetishist, bi-sexual murderer . . . [who] displays considerable deviational overlap. We may get necrophilia too. As a sort of bonus" (*Plays*, 428).
Addressing his diagnosis to Mrs. Prentice, Rance links Prentice's "insanity with primitive religion and asks Prentice why he has turned his back on religion. Prentice declares himself a rationalist, incurring Rance's comment that he "can't be a rationalist in an irrational world. It isn't rational" (*Plays*, 428). Orton's playing around with verbal contradictions takes yet another turn in his use of the term "abnormal normality":

RANCE: (*to Mrs. Prentice*) His belief in normality is quite
             abnormal. (*to Dr. Prentice*) Was the girl killed before
             or after you took her clothes off?

PRENTICE: He wasn't a girl. He was a man.

MRS. P.:   He was wearing a dress.

PRENTICE: He was a man for all that. (*Plays*, 428, 429)

Abnormality as normality or irrationality as rationality illustrate Orton's by now legendary reinvention of axiomatic usage. He spares no authority, even, as in the last quoted line, famous literary allusions that have entered common usage.

Contradictory actions match contradictory linguisms. At a point in the play where any distinctions between fantasy and reality have vanished, Nick finds himself in Sergeant Match's uniform and interrupts Rance's allegations against Prentice to announce that he has just arrested his own brother, Nicholas Beckett (himself). Like Geraldine's earlier attempts at truthfulness, his comments are pounced upon by Rance as fuel for his psychiatric theories.

A mad scene follows in which Mrs. Prentice attempts to force her husband at gunpoint to have sex with her, and, failing to do so, shoots at him. Confusion breaks loose as bodies pile up on the floor, concluding in the mutual threats by Rance and Prentice to certify each other. The madness seems total. Even the blood flowing from the injuries incurred by Nick and Match in the melee is not real to Rance, whose obsession with theorizing only hardens as events feed it. For Nick and Match, the personal consequence is bloody, and for all, the social consequence is the eventual return to the normal order of things, agreed on in the conspiracy among Prentice, Rance, and Match to keep the events out of the papers.

Orton relies on another centuries-old farce convention to unravel the secrets and restore legitimate identities: the use of a trivial object, in this case a brooch. French farceurs, as with Sardou in *A Glass of Water*, regularly used such artifices by which to move the plot or to resolve the confusions in their plays. Shakespeare for his purpose used the handkerchief in *Othello*, and Wilde the handbag in *The Importance of Being Earnest*. Orton's brooch had been broken in two by Mrs. Prentice, each half pinned to a twin. Geraldine and Nick are revealed to be those long-lost twins born to Dr. and Mrs. Prentice as the consequence of their premarital liaison in a cupboard at the Station Hotel. They produce their halves of the brooch given them by their mother when she had to give them up.

Rance is ecstatic as he triumphantly announces a double incest that "is even more likely to produce a best-seller than murder—and this is as it should be for love *must* bring greater joy than violence" (*Plays*, 446). Double incest—Prentice's attempted rape of his daughter and Mrs. Prentice's alleged assault by her son—is beyond even Rance's wildest hopes as a psychiatrist and as a novelist.

Orton has broken boundaries in daring to take his "happy ending" beyond that of the conventional farce. He pronounces no judgment on the violators in the double-incest situation. Indeed, the major villain, Rance, who already profits from imposing his theories on others, will only increase his profits with his lucrative novel. As in the ending of *Loot*—Truscott's conspiracy to share the loot with Hal, Dennis, and Fay—Rance, Prentice, and Match compliment each other on "uncovering a number of remarkable pecadilloes" and promise to "cooperate in keeping them out of the papers" (*Plays*, 448).

Orton's parody of the happy ending is accomplished by not one but several big scenes involving the clearing up of the disguises with the brooch-engendered revelations of the twins' identities and with a second object—the missing part of the Churchill statue. With the latter, the farce returns to its first-act mystery—the contents of Geraldine's box which held the evidence of Geraldine's stepparentage. In his use of both brooch and phallus, Orton doubles Wilde's use of one object, the famous handbag. Match's earlier request that "someone produce or cause to be produced the missing parts of Sir Winston Churchill" (*Plays*, 447) is answered by Geraldine's producing the box with which she had initially arrived for her interview. From this box Match triumphantly lifts "a section from a larger than life-sized bronze statue" (*Plays*, 447). Present at the blowing up of Churchill's statue, the only mother Geraldine had ever known had left her stepdaughter a legacy. Geraldine's assumption that the box she was given at Mrs. Barclay's funeral contained only her mother's clothes is dispelled, and she is proclaimed by Match as "the only living descendant of a woman violated by the hero of 1940" (*Plays*, 447). Orton's devilish trick is the coinciding of Geraldine's personal heritage with that of the nation. Orton's final attack on audience sensibilities occurs in Rance's declaration that blends Churchillian cigar and Ortonian phallus: "How much more inspiring if, in those dark days [World War II] we'd seen what we see now. Instead we had to be content with a cigar—the symbol falling far short, as we all realize, of the object itself" (*Plays*, 447).

Personal, national, and historical occurrences undergo a ritual sanctification in the pagan-Christian scene with which the play closes. Herculean in his leopard-spotted dress, the missing Sergeant Match appears through a skylight in "a great blaze of glory" (*Plays*, 446). The final words, however, are Rance's as all, clothed in their tattered "fig leaves," leave their Edenic frolics and follow Match up the ladder to face the world.

Orton's laughter at the corrupted order of things is complete in its purity, untouched by distracting personal revenge or sympathy with characters (however unintended) as with Wilson in *The Ruffian on the Stair*, Buchanan in *The Good and Faithful Servant*, or McLeavy in *Loot*. A dead mother's eye and false teeth (*Entertaining Mr. Sloane*) and a severed hand (*Funeral Games*) are not present to cause audience unease. The farcical mode is intact throughout. With the distance of time, even the phallus, essential to Orton's antic mode, does not induce the audience unease that accompanies the eye and teeth of earlier plays.

One minor caveat to this total detachment is the bowdlerized ending of the play, when Geraldine looks into the box and sees a cigar rather than a phallus. Even here, however, that ending is canceled by Rance's reference to her identification as an illusion of youth. Aside from the alternate ending—and one that a number of scholars see as an opening of the meaning to various approaches—the play remains uncompromised in its detachment—a feat noticeably taking shape in *The Erpingham Camp* and *Funeral Games* and perfected in *What the Butler Saw*.

Kenneth Williams, an actor in *Loot*, recalls Orton's frequent quoting of "Wilde's dictum: 'Talent is the infinite capacity for taking pains.' He took pains. Polish. Reconstruct. Give you another edition. Another page. Every word polished painstakingly until the whole structure *glitters*" (quoted in Lahr 1978, 202–203). *What the Butler Saw* is Orton's glittering structure line upon line, right up to the very last one by Rance, who parodies Adam's departure from the Garden of Eden with "Let us put on our clothes and face the world" (*Plays*, 448). It is this brilliance of detachment toward which Orton had worked since his prison days.

Wilde's influence is seen in the big revelatory scene as Orton parades characters and actions from *The Importance of Being Earnest*. He transforms Wilde's Canon Chasuble into Dr. Prentice, Miss Prism into Mrs. Prentice, Algernon and Jack into Nick and Geraldine, and the identifying handbag into a similarly functioning brooch. There is even a quick allusion to Wilde's handbag in one of Prentice's many angry retorts to his wife: "Unless you're very careful you'll find yourself in a suitcase awaiting collection" (*Plays*, 393). Orton goes far beyond Wilde, however, in his addition of the character of Rance, whose theories are now to be transformed into a money-making potboiler.

The real success of *What the Butler Saw*, however, lies in Orton's transformation of the characters and situations from earlier plays into a stylistic balancing act heretofore not realized. There are the innocents and the authority figures, both of whom Orton mocks. One character type that continues in *What the Butler Saw* is the pair of innocents who, although victims of others, manage to devictimize themselves mostly by their truth-telling. Their lineage goes back to the two brothers in *The Ruffian on the Stair*, to Hal and Dennis in *Loot*, and the twins in *The Good and Faithful Servant*. Like Hal, Nick and Geraldine attempt to tell the truth whenever an opportunity presents itself, but no one will believe them. They can do little except become caught up in the whirl of events. To the Kath-like Mrs. Prentice, Orton adds a farcical touch of dysfunctional sexuality to the nymphomania both exhibit. There are the two authorities—psychiatrists who are the new religion, Milton's new presbyters as old priests writ large. They resemble the two competitive clerics in *Funeral Games* in their hostility to each other. There is, finally, the Truscott-like Sergeant Match, whose sleuthing here serves as a compounding of the psychiatric sleuthing of Rance. Both proceed with Holmesian deductive methods to put the final touches to the solution of Orton's mysteries.

Any vestiges of Pinteresque intruders are transformed into farcical types that go beyond the satirical stereotypes of earlier plays. Rance and Match carry out their duties in a sublimely unshakable conviction of sexual and professional fantasies, totally oblivious to the realities in which the others are maneuvering their ways in and out of mistaken identities. All are victims of a sort, except for Rance, who remains at the end as he was in the beginning—untouched by events.

Unlike Orton's other plays, *What the Butler Saw* contains no murders or deaths, no personal revenge. The emphasis on revenge is transformed into one on madness. The catalyst for the transformation is the sexual energy that drives Prentice and the passion that drives the theories of Rance. The phallic instinct embraces a wide variety of sexual experiences—for instance, heterosexuality, homosexuality, transvestism, rape, incest.

Orton seems to have exorcised family figures and relationships in his earlier work, so that they do not exist as important sources for the characters anymore. His father and mother—haunting the characters of Kath and Kemp in *Entertaining Mr. Sloane*, Buchanan in *The Good and Faithful Servant*, and McLeavy in *Loot*—have vanished. Although, like Elsie and John Orton, the Prentices live separate lives, Mrs. Prentice's active engagement in sexual liaisons at the Station Hotel go far beyond the attempts of Mrs. Orton merely to make herself physically attractive. Furthermore, Mrs. Prentice's actions serve more as a farcical doubling to move the plot than as a characterization technique. Sex itself is treated

only partly in the manner of a traditional farce—like a Feydeau character's bumbling to disguise the *idea* of indiscretion rather than the literal
action. There is one exception—Mrs. Prentice, whose sexual escapade
with Nick is not only real but also, as asserted in a comment by Rance,
natural. Another autobiographical detail prominent in earlier plays—the
garden and floral imagery associated with William Orton—functions
only as a minor mover of the plot rather than as developer of character.
Prentice tries desperately to hide incriminating evidence in a vase from
which roses have to be moved repeatedly to hide a new indiscretion.

Most important, Orton has finally exorcised the personal need to
offend audience sensibilities, having already done so explicitly in actions
such as Ed's and Kath's sharing of Sloane or of Hal's disturbing viola-
tions of his mother's body. With all elements of his farce—real and unre-
al—existing in proportion to each other, his outrage still energizes the
actions, but it does so in hilarious complications that grow dizzyingly
from one man's—Prentice's—phallic instinct. Mechanically, the plot
begins and ends with a phallus carried on stage in Geraldine's box. A
symbol as old as Aristophanes' *Lysistrata*, the phallus is nature's force
against destructive authority—Aristophanes' target being the insanity of
war.

Orton's earlier attacks on religion, law, politics, and corporate
parentalism come together in his final battle with authority. His lifelong
war began in *Head to Toe*, with the character of Gombold, who learns to
use words to rage correctly. Although Rance, unlike the giant, lives, his
creator's verbal weaponry has hit its mark with unprecedented farcical
accuracy.

Orton's attacks on Rance expose fashionably glib theories that, in
the context in which they are expressed, are as mad as Rance's obsession
to impose them automatically on the events he witnesses. His observations drawn from the seemingly endless changes of dress prompt him to
conclude that Prentice is a pervert, "a man who mauls young boys,
importunes policemen and lives on terms of intimacy with a woman
who shaves twice a day" (*Plays*, 417). When Prentice informs his wife
that he has given his secretary the sack, she concludes that he has killed
Geraldine and put her body into a sack. Her comments lead Rance, in
a series of logical leaps, to link Prentice to primitive religions. Prentice's
response to Rance's further accusations of atheism is that he is a rationalist, eliciting from Rance one of the play's most often repeated lines:
"You can't be a rationalist in an irrational world. It isn't rational" (*Plays*,
428).

As Orton's spokesman for contemporary theories, Rance in his madness is endowed with financial preoccupations. He concludes with a reference to his "documentary type 'novelette'" that should reap "twelve record-breaking reprints. I'll be able to leave the service of the Commissioners and bask in the attentions of those who, like myself, find other people's iniquity puts money in their purse" (*Plays*, 424–25).

In contrast, the behavior of Prentice, at first more farcically human than psychiatrically insane, is rapidly energized into a madness of its own, swept on by the passionate intensity with which Rance leaps from personal and societal levels to anthropological significance. Rance refers at one point to "the startling ideas of Dr. Goebbels on the function of the male sexual organ" from which "we pass quite logically to white golliwogs. An attempt, in fact, to change the order of creation—homosexuality slots in here—dabbling in the black arts! The reported theft of the private parts of a well-known public figure ties in with this theory. We've phallic worship under our noses or I'm a Dutchman" (*Plays*, 424). With one brilliant structural ploy, Orton links Rance's insanity with a detail with which the play opens—the contents of the box with which Geraldine enters Prentice's office. It is this detail with which Orton resolves the complications created by Prentice and Rance.

The circularity of Orton's farcical plot remains intact and the object of his satire—psychiatric insanity—remains firmly in place to the end. Katharine Worth writes of a correspondence between the madness in Orton's play and the earnestness in Wilde's *The Importance of Being Earnest*. Both are the "root vice of the play; all the other ills are seen branching out from it" (Worth, 81). She also points out an adverse truth that she regards as the central joke of Orton's plot: that the "invented identities turn out to be after all, the true ones" (Worth, 81). As a result of the disguises foisted on them, Nick and Geraldine do turn out to be in reality closer to their invented selves than they or anyone else had imagined—all of this the result of Prentice's indiscretion, the "original sin" of the play. They experience the sexual decompartmentalization of which Orton has often spoken, as realities within fantasies and truths within lies abound in the play. The punch and counterpunch of sanity and insanity momentarily liberate even as they create the wild plot complications and eventually establish family relationships.

Worth views the farce, despite its many similarities to Wilde, to the Aldwych tradition, or to the standard French farce, as a bacchanalian dream to which an end is put by the deus ex machina but also a dream that gives both "a great id-releasing experience and a reassuring demonstration of the power of wit to control it" (Worth, 84). The darkness consists in the fantasies that underlie life, and it is the balance between these fantasies and life that results in health. Like Alice's bottle instructions—"Drink Me"—farce as antidote threatens as possible poison but ultimately frees. Worth uses as a case in point Geraldine Barclay, who never grasps Prentice's overtures as seduction attempts. Her failure to do so results in her breaking up "into a number of different selves" (Worth, 80). Transformation after transformation occurs as the secretary is hunted by Mrs. Prentice, Rance, and Match. The released spirits of secretary and hotel page, created by their changes of clothes, float freely as shapes for the "real characters to go in and out of." Their real identities as illegitimate children are the result of the freeing of the id. Orton said that his aim in *What the Butler Saw* (as in *Loot*) was to "break down all the sexual compartments people have" (quoted in Gordon, 91).

Maurice Charney has cataloged the compartments in the farce as "all possible varieties of sexual behaviour, buggery, necrophilia, exhibitionism, hermaphroditism, rape, sadomasochism, fetishism, transvestism, nymphomania and the triumphant mock-Wildean recognition scene, in which sexual fulfillment awaits the 'bleeding, drugged and drunk' characters'" (Charney, 101–102). He might have added to his list Orton's favorite id-releasor—one he proudly records in his *Diaries* and was, he claims, borrowed from *Entertaining Mr. Sloane* by Pinter in *The Homecoming*—the sharing of sexual partners.

Both Worth and Charney call attention to the parodic title of Orton's last play. Unfettered by the presence of the requisite butler, the play is about what the butler may have seen had Orton, indeed, included such a character. Worth notes that not one of the characters sees a given situation as does another, so that all free-float in their respective ways, each unrestricted by views of another. The experiences of the missing butler and the play's characters can be extended to individual members of any given audience who may experience similar liberation.

Charney brings a historical perspective to his views of Orton's farce with references to sources and analogues that begin with the play from which Orton has lifted the epigraph—Tourneur's *The Revenger's Tragedy*, one of the "most extravagant of seventeenth-century black comedies . . . a play much influenced by Shakespeare's *Hamlet*" (Charney, 98). He attributes the turning of the play, as in *Hamlet*, on the matter of the missing father, with the resulting connection with incest and other odd matters of sexual satisfaction. Beyond Tourneur and Shakespeare, there is Orton's replacement of satire with saturnalia, which provides a "comic release from the burdens of sexual identity" (Charney, 100). This, Charney points out, reflects Orton's combination of the virtues of the old and new farce—"tumultuous sexual energy of Aristophanes, the careful intrigue plotting of Plautus" (Charney, 107). These Greek, Roman, and Renaissance characteristics coexist with the black comedy styles of Beckett, Pinter, Ionesco, Stoppard, and especially Brecht.

The specific Tourneuresque qualities identified by Charney are the "bizarre and unanticipatable shifts in tone" and the "almost hysterically rhetorical" flights, so that the designation of the play as tragedy is justified only "by certain technicalities of its endings" (Charney, 98). Those technicalities—in general the return of nighttime dreams to daytime realities and specifically the blood spilling and tattered clothing—seem at odds with the farcical tone of the rest of the play. Yet they can be seen as much more than "technicalities."

Detailed Jacobean assimilations are dealt with by William Hutchings, who asserts that it is the influence of this literary period that "supersedes [that of] all other sources and analogues." He notes, first of all, the "inherent theatricality of madness"[3] that is so much a part of Renaissance tradition, beginning with the real madness of Hieronymo in Kyd's *The Spanish Tragedy* (1586) and with the title character's feigned madness in *Hamlet* (1602). Hutchings draws a picture of the psychiatrist's office as the "modern counterpart of the Jacobean stage's Italianate court," where, "amid elaborate intrigues, disguises, and self-serving duplicities—all sorts of passions and lusts, however forbidden or illicit, flourish outside any norms of moral judgment, unrestrained by social taboos and regarded with clinical detachment by both perpetrators and authorities in charge" (Hutchings, 229). The revelations of young women to be men and men to be women are those found, respectively, in Jonson's *Epicoene* (1609) and in Beaumont and Fletcher's *Philaster* (1610) and Shakespeare's *Twelfth Night* (1602). In few periods has incest been so prevalent a dramatic theme as in the seventeenth century: John Ford's *'Tis a Pity She's a Whore* (1627), Beaumont and Fletcher's *A King and No King* (1611), and Middleton's *Women, Beware Women* (1623).

In his reference to the unsettling shift in tone in the ending of Orton's farce, Hutchings recalls a reverse shifting of tone, not unlike Orton's, in the unusually harsh punishments in Ben Jonson's *Volpone* (1605). Neither Jonson nor Orton relates to "any righting of a 'moral balance,'" nor in either is justice meted out fairly "since equally 'guilty' characters do not suffer alike" (Hutchings, 231). Hutchings refers to the asylums in Rowley and Middleton's *The Changeling* (1622)—asylums run by Alibius

and Lollio much as those run by Prentice and Rance. Hutchings emphasizes Orton's insistence on the copious blood shed by Nick and Match—
a detail euphemized in some productions. With bloodshed as the essence
of Jacobean tragedy, Orton's insistence on it, despite the discomfiting
shift in style, is in order. It is there even in *The Erpingham Camp*, a television farce with a style similar to that of *What the Butler Saw*. What
makes Orton's kinships with influences different from those, for example, in the plays of Tom Stoppard are Orton's cunning concealing of
them so that they unify the play "in ways that were not apparent to its
earliest reviewers" and in so doing justify "the seemingly inapposite
bloodshed" (Hutchings, 234). It is this inapposition that Charney dismisses and that Hutchings regards importantly as part of Orton's daring
"to outrage conventional proprieties" (Hutchings, 234).

Beyond all the influences or analogues linked with Orton's plays,
what places Orton's genius in a category by itself is what Leslie Smith
refers to as the medieval feast of fools—the brief carnival period that
preceded the restoration of order. Farce has, until Orton, assumed the
rightness of that order. Orton has written his name into dramatic history by his dissension with the traditional farce ending, nowhere more
hilarious and dark than in *What the Butler Saw*. In his "modern and
uncompromising vision, that feast of fools, in all its grotesqueness and
licence, [Orton] offers a permanent image of the human condition, not a
temporary one."[4]

Orton refuses to cleanse and restore the body politic. He chooses
merely to continue the status quo—reality's outrage, as he has stated.
Furthermore, he has done so by writing subversively in a language that
Hilary Spurling says gives the impression of being a foreign language,
one that "for all its sharp intelligence and formal polish, . . . is firmly
rooted in the shabby, baggy catchphrases of contemporary speech;
[Orton is] almost alone among contemporary playwrights" (Spurling,
344).

One of few dissenting voices about the relative merits of *What the
Butler Saw* is John Russell Taylor, who, having lauded *Entertaining Mr.
Sloane* as a comedy of manners and *Loot* as a parody of the detective
genre, sees *What the Butler Saw* as less successful than Orton's other
plays, primarily on the basis of the absence of a norm (or a straight man)
on which the very idea of farce rests. Consequently, in his view the play
"soon becomes reduced to a succession of lines and happenings in a total
vacuum" (Taylor, 138). Taylor then qualifies his stance as a possibly
unfair one in "taking apart a play which comes to us in what we may

presume to be an extremely provisional form" (Taylor, 139). Orton, having been irked by Taylor's earlier references to *Entertaining Mr. Sloane* as commercial entertainment, had he been alive, would have been even more irritated with Taylor's extension of the commercial label to *What the Butler Saw*.

In 1995 the stage history of *What the Butler Saw* came full circle, from its failed premiere at a West End theater in 1969, through subsequent successes at the Royal Court Theatre in 1975 and at New York's Manhatan Theater Club in 1989, to the ultimate honor—a production at one of England's two most prestigious theaters, the Royal National Theatre. Three seasoned critics pose interesting contrasts in their evaluations, all referring to the 1969 disaster. Irving Wardle, who admitted to eating his words about 1969 yet holding reservations about 1975, now judged the first act of the 1995 production to be sublime and John Alderton's running of the "the longest gag in living memory" to be a guarantee of this revival's holding "a permanent place in the Orton annals."[5] Even reluctant Benedict Nightingale, like Wardle "a *Loot* fan," seemed to look mostly for an explanation of why the "gales of laughter" ended as "blustery gusts."[6] Michael Billington, however, noted the production's (Phyllida Lloyd's) "absolute understanding of Orton's peculiar mix of verbal precision and sexual anarchy," of his "ability to depict gathering chaos with algebraic precision and Wildean finesse," and of his skill in escalating the frenzy of "authority disintegrating into panic."[7] As bedraggled characters "ascend skywards on Mark Thompson's glittering golden platform, it is as if the world of farcical mayhem has suddenly been invaded by Euripides and sixties satire has mated with *The Bacchae*." To Billington's comment one may add that the 1960s turbulences in *What the Butler Saw* reach into those of seventeenth-century Britain as well as Euripides' time, all three periods marked by social and political upheavals.

Chapter Nine
A Final Trick: A Matter of the Emperor's Clothes

In *What the Butler Saw* Orton pulled from his bag of farceur's tricks two consummate metaphors for his war on society. The images of the coffin in *Loot* and the "ton of smokeless" in *Funeral Games* are added to in the seemingly harmless boxes carried by Geraldine and Nick in this, Orton's last play. Retrospectively, their contents—Churchillian phallus and Herculean costume—constitute Orton's farewell image to a stage world that in its own tumultuous way had finally acknowledged his talent. Throughout the frenzied actions of *What the Butler Saw*, Geraldine's box contains the quiescent phallus of Sir Winston Churchill's statue. Metaphorically it represents the phallic eruption that begins early in the opening scene. Literally it remains boxed until the final scene when Match frees it and holds it up in triumphant confirmation of the sexual transformations that have occurred throughout. The dress in Nick's box also functions in a double capacity, stylistically as a physical disguise, part of farce convention, and thematically as Bacchic escape from repressive sexual norms. Dress and phallus unite at the end as Match, attired in the dress, exposes the phallus to the full view of the audience.

The dress is only one of a number of disguises in Orton's veritable Mardi Gras of costume changes that take on significances not present in earlier plays, where costumes exist for satirical and naturalistic purposes. Sloane's leather pants are merely a part of the comfortable life to which he aspires. Buchanan's uniform is an only too obvious image of the meaningless uniformity of a corporate-determined life. Mrs. McLeavy's shoes, dress, and fur that Fay appropriates as her rightful loot for services rendered to the McLeavy family provide satiric commentary on her greed. McCorquodale's complaint of the discomfort of the clerical collar functions similarly as satire. In *What the Butler Saw*, however, items of apparel drive the plot, beginning immediately with Geraldine's shedding of her underwear and continuing with the alternate shedding and donning of Nick's hotel page uniform, Geraldine's dress, Mrs. Prentice's leopard-spotted dress, an inspector's uniform, and, importantly, the straitjacket by which one mad psychiatrist attempts to imprison those who fit his preordained definition of insanity.

Normally a means of confining a character to a socially prescribed role, clothes here serve both to drive the plot mechanics and to create a Bacchic release of natural impulses in response to the Pentheus-like authoritarian figures of Prentice and Rance. In tattered condition at the end, clothes join bleeding bodies as part of Orton's unnerving conclusion involving the return to a corrupt normality—its criminality evidenced in the conspiratorial agreement among all to keep the events that have transpired hidden from the public, much like the endings of *The Erpingham Camp* and *Loot*.

Clothing changes, however magnificently they release imprisoned sexual identities, are a metaphor for a release of another sort—language itself. Inventively using mannered speech to rid itself of its flagrantly hypocritical usage, Orton creates fresh, epigrammatic language patterns that are his literary hallmark. In his attempted seduction of an attractive interviewee, Prentice sets in motion not only an unheralded release of dreamlike, free-floating sexual selves but also the verbal counterparts of those selves. Aphorisms are re-created in newly minted epigrams, their freshness emanating from the distance between the words and the situation to which those words apply. Like Gombold's learning the right words to cause a seismic shift in the dead giant he inhabits (*Head to Toe*), Orton's mastery of verbal images, at their height in *What the Butler Saw*, caused theater earthquakes, his giant being middle-class Churchillian England. Appropriately, Orton's success during his lifetime occurred in the middle of one of the most socially turbulent decades of the twentieth century—specifically, 1965, the year of Churchill's death.

In *What the Butler Saw*, as in no previous Orton play, disguises serve to liberate both characters and language. In other plays selves remain imprisoned in their linguistic disguises. For example, in *The Ruffian on the Stair* there is Joyce's polite blandness in her reaction to a scandalous suggestion when Mike informs her that he is going to meet a man in the toilet at King's Cross Station: "You always go to such interesting places" (*Plays*, 31). With similarly empty politeness, Mike explains to Wilson, when he asks the latter to leave, the reason for the request, "It's embarrassing to be ill in a stranger's presence" (*Plays*, 51). Wilson, as a potential roomer, zenophobically confesses to Joyce, "I'm not coloured; I was brought up in the Home counties" (*Plays*, 33). The wit, perhaps, is all the more scathingly subversive for its distance from underlying realities.

It is but a presaging of the dark humor that at times takes on a life of its own as the very raison d'être for the play.

The ferocity of Orton's satiric attack on hypocrisy—for Orton a type of pornography—intensifies in each play. He attacks middle-class concern with appearances in Sloane's memories of his parents who, he tells Kath, may have died in a suicide pact: "From what I remember they was respected. You know, H.P. debts, a little light gardening. The usual activities of a cultured community. I respect them" (*Plays*, 68). Kath's views are no less unenlightened in her condemnation of a neighbor for an immorality vaguely suggestive of her own guilty concern about neighborly gossip. A daughter of a neighbor is involved in a court case that vaguely echoes Kath's fear-ridden guilt about her own illegitimate pregnancies. With Pinteresque insecurity, she complains to Sloane, "She tells everybody her business. . . . Tells every detail. . . . Oh, if only I had been born without ears" (*Plays*, 78).

Affectations of common speech, especially vulnerable to Orton's satire, expose as well those institutions fostering pretentiousness, with law and religion among the most conspicuous. Eddie, for example, is generous in giving the murderer of two men (one of them his own father) another chance: "Your youth pleads for leniency, and, by God, I'm going to give it. You're pure as the lamb. Purer" (*Plays*, 120). Manners and decorum are dealt a blow in comments such as Eddie's to Kath about the dilemma of Sloane's fate: "You're on the horns of it" (*Plays*, 145). Word affectations such as "conception" permeate some of Orton's most damning lines as in Eddie's rejection of Kath's plea for the presence of Sloane at the birth of their child: "It's all any reasonable child can expect if the dad is present at the conception. Let's hear no more of it" (*Plays*, 149). A lower-key version of the same situation, but without the use of the actual word, occurs when Buchanan (*The Good and Faithful Servant*) comments on the anonymity of his grandson's father, whose morality must have been below average, when, in fact, he himself has just learned of the child he had fathered by Edith, the scrubwoman in the factory from which he has just retired. Yet another conception-centered line occurs in McLeavy's regret at having fathered Hal: "I'd have withheld myself at his conception if I'd known" (*Plays*, 264).

It is in *Loot*, however, that Orton's wit takes wing and flies with a speed that can keep an audience playing catch-up with the lines. In one short introductory scene, Fay and McLeavy recite asocial sentiments in approved middle-class jargon, sentiments about the dead Mrs. McLeavy's fur, slippers, and gown, and even a replacement (Fay herself) for the dead wife—the last-mentioned idea, according to Fay, being treated as a challenge, "a Catholic problem" by Mother Agnes-Mary. In a fresh Ortonesque turn of a cliché, Fay criticizes McLeavy's private grief and admonishes Hal to show his "emotions in public or not at all" (*Plays*, 108). And there is Dennis's questioning of Hal's truthfulness in answering questions: "Why can't you lie like a normal man? (*Plays*, 207).

But it is Truscott and the criminality of the law at whom Orton's wit is aimed most lethally. In proof of Orton's dictum that all classes are criminal, Truscott, when Fay suspects him, engages her in a name-signing exercise that he may have occasion to use later on a trumped-up charge of forgery. Having related to Fay the details of her murders of seven husbands, he then advises her to avoid the attentions of Dennis, who is not her type and who has five pregnancies to his credit. After kicking Hal violently and knocking him to the floor, he shouts, "Under any other system, I'd have you on the floor in tears" (*Plays*, 235). Truscott's attempt to pin another murder on Fay is but one illustration of an Ortonesque epigram about the irrationality of being rational in an irrational world. He insists that he and Mrs. McLeavy are "the two people most closely involved in her death. I'd be interested to hear her on the subject" (*Plays*, 252). In another of his twisted edicts, Truscott, having just handcuffed McLeavy, responds to the latter's request to see a higher authority: "You can see whoever you like, providing you convince me first that you're justified in seeing them" (*Plays*, 274). In an ending that has become a signature of Orton's plays, all four collude in McLeavy's imprisonment on murder charges and in agreeing on his "accidental" death in prison. Truscott's smiling departure is followed by admiring words from Hal and Dennis, the former comforted by the fact that "the police can still be relied upon when we're in trouble" (*Plays*, 275). Fay's hypocrisy concludes the play as she returns to silent prayer, with Dennis and Hal on either side of the coffin. For the four criminals, the ending is a happy one.

Although language undergoes transformation in *Loot*, physical clothes maintain their naturalistic/satiric function throughout. In *What the Butler Saw* dress joins language in the transformational process, sharpening the lethal outrageousness of the language. Linguistic clothing here is that of the educated class and, particularly, the fashionable jargon of the prevailing religion—psychiatry. In word and deed, the emperor begins the shedding of clothes early in Prentice's panic-induced comparison of his wife's nymphomania with the Holy Grail—wife and Grail are "ardently sought after by young men" (*Plays*, 368)—and prepares the audience for the increasingly irreverent epigrammatic turns that follow. Out of context, Orton's lines may read like gags. In context, they are integral to the plot and to the theme of Bacchic release. When Mrs. Prentice, attempting to bribe Nicholas for incriminating photographs, reacts to his demand for a hundred pounds and a position as her husband's secretary, she accuses him of putting her in an impossible position. She is met with his low-life pun that "no position is impossible when you're young and healthy" (*Plays*, 370). Mrs. Prentice's claims to "bogus uterine contractions" evoke a fashionable reaction from her husband: "What a discovery! Married to a mistress of the fraudulent climax" (*Plays*, 372). When she attempts to convince Prentice to hire Nicholas, she speaks of the latter's "failure in commerce. That's why he took to rape" (*Plays*, 375). The revelation of her Oedipal incest, unrecognized as such at the time, is followed shortly by Rance's introduction to Prentice as a representative of Her Majesty's government and, as such, the latter's "immediate superior in madness" (*Plays*, 376). In all its madness, psychological cant at this point is taken over by Rance and, in consort with the panic-driven changes in disguises, propels the action to the bloody mayhem of one of the several climactic scenes of the farce.

Moving beyond the vulgarly middle-class world of the Kemps in *Entertaining Mr. Sloane* and the slightly more respectable class of nurses and inspectors in *Loot* to the upper-middle class of psychiatrists, Orton retains the socially lower cast of characters, but they exist in the context of their social superiors, where they function in another world, not as characters who make naturalistic choices but ones who are spun into other worlds. They are propelled by situational exigencies over which they have no control yet which allow them the liberation of a dream in which their identities are split, multiplied, dissolved, and merged, as in, for example, the most famous of dream plays, Strindberg's *A Dream Play*. In Orton's dream anything can and does happen, as characters are freed temporarily from the oppressive responsibilities of their waking lives—for instance, Geraldine's and Nick's job-hunting. Their wit is similarly given unrestricted freedom to examine a litany of liberating fantasies. It remains for *What the Butler Saw* to transform the criminality of language into heights of realized fantasies yet add to that criminality the violence of tattered clothing and bloodshed that besmirch the otherwise "happy endings" that are the lot (excepting McLeavy) of the characters in *Loot*. The boundaries for anarchic impulses are set only by the strict discipline of farce conventions, consisting here mainly of objects (the two boxes that complicate and unravel the plot), a rapidity of exits and entrances, and, of course, disguises.

Words match actions with an aesthetically satisfying consistency. Formulaic plot details, which begin normally enough with the convergence of a job interview and the interviewer's sexual urgency, soon turn abnormal as other details that include the psychiatrist's couch, and, thematically important, the phallus and leopard-spotted dress, are used by Orton to invent a new kind of happy ending. As in Gogol's play *The Inspector General* and his novel *Dead Souls*, the identity confusions become fantasies that take on a life of their own for the time allotted them within the time of the dream. In Gogol's world offenders are exposed and exiled; in Orton's they remain, their only punishment tattered clothes and bleeding bodies.

To link the outrageously unlikely subjects of a statue of Churchill, the North Thames Gas Board, and Mrs. Barclay's death, Orton uses one of the most common of farcical situations—an amorous employer interviewing a young secretary in search of her first job. Prentice's response to the story of her stepmother's death at first may seem like a gag line, but from it emanates the free-wheeling wit with which similarly incongruous situations are met. In a perfectly professional tone, Prentice says, "You've had a unique experience. It's not everyone that has their stepmother assassinated by the North Thames Gas Board" (*Plays*, 365). When Geraldine is given her chance to express a sentiment in response to Prentice's account of his unhappy marriage, she agrees to testing his new contraceptive device, removes her underclothes, and expresses her delight at being able to help him in any way she can. In successive episodes this opening scene explodes into fragments of itself, each releasing sexual fantasies of anarchic proportions. From the mundane inefficiency of the Thames Gas Board, incongruities follow each other with all the disorder of the dream/nightmare reality of an Alice-like Wonderland.

Prentice, having already violated professional standards, orders the naked Geraldine to hide behind the screen: "You have my word as a gentleman" (*Plays*, 400). To her reminder of his professed interest only in her mind, he assures her that "that's like 'open sesame'—a formula for gaining entrance" (*Plays*, 404). Prentice's desperation carries him to irrationally rational depths when, under suspicion of assault on Match, he decides: "I'm suspected of the offense, I might as well commit it" (*Plays*, 420). Anticipating Rance's misinterpretation of yet another change of clothes, Prentice fears having to account for the disappearance of both secretary and page-boy, so he refutes Geraldine's argument that in their current dress these do not exist: "When people who don't exist disappear, the account of their departure must be convincing" (*Plays*, 419). And in a convoluted conversation with Nick about Nick's service as a "slave of a corporal in the Welsh Fusiliers," Rance concludes, "A case of opening the stable after the horse is in" (*Plays*, 433). Witty action and language are one in their released states as in none of the earlier plays. Rance's part in this celebration of freedom caps the high jinks of the others. Deluded, as the others are not, he questions Mrs. Prentice's seeing of naked men: "When did these delusions start?" (*Plays*, 422).

What additional liberating tricks of farce Orton may have pulled will remain in his bag. Less than a month before his death, he recorded in his diaries his pleasure at the Euripidean ending of *What the Butler Saw*, stressing "the leopard-spotted dress for Match." Relieved at the completion of the play, he wrote, "I can now give my mind full rein for the historical farce set on the eve of Edward VII's coronation in 1902 and called (at the moment) *Prick up Your Ears*" (*Diaries*, 242). His debt to Halliwell ironically continues in his expressed hope that he "could write a play worthy of one of Kenneth Halliwell's brilliant titles" (242). The title, of course, was appropriated by Lahr for his biography of Orton.

With his inclusion of England's historical giant of the twentieth century as a part of the scandalous actions of *What the Butler Saw*, one can only speculate on the irreverence with which Orton would have approached Edwardian mores. Moving up the social ladder from his early treatments of lower-middle-class life to the middle-class world of educated professionals, he would now have entered a stage world he had already written about in his Edwardian skit, *Until She Screams* (for Kenneth Tynan's "*Oh, Calcutta!*"). Orton even had in mind a quotation from Sheridan's *The Critic*: "Where history gives you a good outline for a play, you may fill up with a little love at your own discretion; in doing which, nine times out of ten, you only make up a deficiency in the private history of the times" (*Diaries*, 242–43). The jump from his own time, the 1960s, to a highly contained one, dictated outwardly by manners and inwardly by a privileged disregard for morals, possibly would have marked a new direction for Orton. His rectifying of history's deficiency would have involved a time when traditional gentility held sway before the onslaughts of the infamous welfare-state gentility of his plays. On 30 July 1967, ten days before his death, he wrote of walking about Brighton thinking "a lot about *Prick Up Your Ears*" (*Diaries*, 264).

Each of his three long plays is a signpost in his development as a play-wright—one a comedy of manners; the second a comedy of horrors as Orton labeled it; and the third a black farce in which crudity of subject matter and elegance of style are wedded with unqualified success. The projected title of his never-to-be-written next play, *Prick Up Your Ears*, is an indicator of the greater freedom he would have exercised had he lived. For him, the title would be a return to the long series of offensive titles he and Halliwell had used or contemplated in their early days: *Priapus in the Shrubbery, Between Us Girls, Up Against It, Until She Screams*, and, as well, the titles he had inserted into a collection of Emlyn Williams's plays in the Islington library: *Knickers Must Fall, Up the Front, Up the Back*, and *Olivia Prude*, among others (Lahr 1978, 81).

With the 1968 passage of the Theatres Act, which freed the theater from the blue pencil of the Lord Chamberlain, a censorship that began in Fielding's time with the Theatres Act of 1737 (amended by the Theatres Act of 1843), more than 200 years of detested stage restrictions came to an end. By 1967, the year of Orton's death, even the bland Wolfenden Report of 1956—in which the Lord Chamberlain had eased the restrictions on homosexuality on the stage if the subject were treated seriously and sincerely—had at least awakened the theatergoing public to a minimal acceptance of a tasteful treatment of the love that dared not speak its name. Both the act and the report, however, were slow in their implementation. Large numbers of dramatists, Rattigan and Osborne among them, faced the threat of potential censorship, despite, in Osborne's case, the presence of private theater societies—the English Stage Company at the Royal Court Theatre the most famous—to perform otherwise forbidden material.

However brief his career as a successful playwright, Orton has made for himself an indelible name in the history of British drama of the twentieth century. Bigsby places Orton in the philosophical context of an age dominated by a sense of metaphysical absurdity more like that of the French than the English. He sees Orton as a dramatist who began as an "exemplar of the former [Pinter] mode, [who] ended as an embodiment of the latter [Beckett]" (Bigsby, 53). Orton's world is one whose "characters move uncertainly or even obliviously through a strange landscape whose strangeness must simply be accepted. This is the world of Beckett's and Pinter's plays, as it is of Stoppard's *Rosencrantz and Guildenstern Are Dead*. It is also the world created by Joe Orton, who actually lived out the absurdity of his age, an age he could never take

entirely seriously but which always threatened to devolve into violence
and death—as, eventually, it did in reality for him" (Bigsby, 52).

Orton, indeed, was alert to the naturalistic absurdities of his own life
and age—an existentialist view that, when unblinkingly sustained,
extends that naturalism to a metaphysical level. Orton's detached enjoyment of his absurdity comes into sharp focus in his diary depictions of his
stalking for sex in dark lavatories. The translation of his own life-style
into the farce of *What the Butler Saw* may, in fact, place him closer to
Genet than to Beckett. Like Genet, Orton was a practitioner of the dark,
id-releasing laws of nature, but, like Beckett, he was a celebrant of the
feast of fools that is life.

Charney, responding to Taylor's early assessment of Orton as a dramatist who is "entitled to at least a footnote in even the severest histories in
our time," comments on Orton's growing popularity and suggests that
he "merits at least a significant chapter" (Charney, 131). To Charney, the
Ortonesque is the quality of the ironist who is constantly alert to the
vulgarity, greed, and lust that peep through the mask of manners, no
matter how elegant the expression of those manners (Charney, 123,
124). The polite vulgarity of which Orton makes art consists of "empty,
conventionalised formulae—slogans, proverbs, advertising copy, political
shibboleths, and all the other verbal junk of a liberal democratic society"
(Charney, 126). The Ortonesque, finally, is "a vigorous assertion of hedo-
nistic self-indulgence, polymorphous perversity and freedom from all
cant" (Charney, 131). Charney's and Bigsby's views, with their different
approaches—one historical and the other stylistic—confirm each other
as to the merits of Orton's work.

Christopher Innes concludes that Orton's plays are morality plays,
despite their "anti-moral stance on one level."[1] In Orton's world, "ethical principles are merely counterfeit, propaganda lies propping up an
immoral society" (Innes, 278). The extreme to which he carries out his
inversion of socially accepted morality qualifies his brand of farce "not so
much subversive, as a declaration of war. It embodies the anarchy it celebrates" (Innes, 278).

Leslie Smith writes of Orton's "significant development of the farce
form, his uncompromising vision of "that feast of fools, in all its
grotesqueness and licence, [that] offers a permanent image of the human
condition, not a temporary one" (Smith, 138). A master farceur, Orton
constructs "dizzying edifices of plot, card-castles of intrigue which finally collapse on the builders" (Smith, 137). As fools dancing between the
social norms of human behavior and the chaos of natural instincts,

Orton's characters literally embody the dance, as in the farcical funeral cortege accident of *Loot*, the games that turn violent in *The Erpingham Camp*, the murderous shenanigans of two clerics in *Funeral Games*, and the mayhem of shootings in *What the Butler Saw*. The truth of the permanence of man's absurd entrapment between two worlds is uttered by one of Orton's most famous criminals, Truscott, who, in response to McLeavy's "Is the world mad? Tell me it's not," informs him that "I'm not paid to quarrel with accepted facts" (*Plays*, 158).

Orton's view of farce as "originally . . . very close to tragedy" that "differed only in the treatment of its themes"[2] is put forth by most critics. Yet, however Aristophanic or Plautine the roots of Orton's farce, its combination of death with life or of horror with laughter constructs a world that conscience and morality have abandoned. In their place presides the amoral order of the dream world, Euripidean in its lawless celebration of the anarchic id, thus the Bacchic frenzy symbolized by Orton's last two farcical tricks—phallus and leopard-spotted dress—which leave a bleeding Pentheus as the consequence of the disorder.

Worth disputes Lahr's tendency to orient his interpretations of Orton's work toward social commentary. In comparing Orton with Wilde, she views his plays as the working out of "dark fantasies in extravagant cosmic terms that both express and exorcise them," thus pushing "the dark elements so much to the fore without losing that sense of health spoken by Lady Bracknell: 'Health is the primary duty of Life'" (Worth, 76). In concluding from Match's final putting on of clothes and facing the world that the farce is "a great id-releasing experience and a reassuring demonstration of the power of wit to control it" (Worth, 84), however, she minimizes Orton's advice to directors, particularly in connection with productions of *Loot*, that at some point laughter stops and horror takes over.

It is this ironic horror of Jacobean drama that Hutchings sees as akin to that in Orton's plays. He reconciles the incongruous bloodshed and the farcical madness in *What the Butler Saw* in his allusions to the motifs and conventions of the Elizabethan stage as exhibited in the dramas of Tourneur, Kyd, Jonson, Beaumont and Fletcher, Rowley and Middleton, Ford, and, of course, Shakespeare. In consequence, Hutchings pairs Orton with Tom Stoppard as the two playwrights who write "with more conscious awareness of the literary traditions" (Hutchings, 228) within which they work than have any other of their contemporaries. A major difference between Orton and Stoppard is that the former's indebtedness is "cunningly concealed in surprisingly congruent twentieth-century counterparts," whereas the latter in his "assimilations of *Hamlet* in *Rosencrantz and Guildenstern Are Dead* and of *'Tis a Pity She's a Whore* in *The Real Thing* are openly acknowledged within the plays themselves" (Hutchings, 234).

So Orton's small opus invites an open-ended variety of approaches—historical, comparative, tragical, farcical, Freudian, sociological, linguistic—whatever a given critic's peculiar orientation may be. In this respect, his plays remain distinct from those of Stoppard and Pinter. Stoppard is an elitist farceur of philosophical intellectualism and Pinter the inscrutable ironist of psychological realities—both, like Orton, easily identified by their inventive stage language. Orton, among the three, is the observer of life on its largest stage. From his oft-referred-to gutter, he has looked up and seen society as the great whore she is and nature as the host at a feast society proscribes. Like Aristophanes, Euripides, the Elizabethans, and a host of modern writers, Orton remains accessible to all, with, perhaps, the exception of the society-concocted Edna Welthorpes.

Lahr's view of Orton as the clown who combines terror with elation and crudity with elegance—"an irresistible amalgam of the highfalutin and the low comic, as in Mrs. Prentice's 'My uterine contractions have been bogus for some time'" (Lahr 1994, 106)—contains within its purview the approaches to Orton's work from which all others emanate. It is the laughter of the clown in the disguise he chooses as his means to lampoon the audience with itself, even as he entertains, that partakes of the dance of life in both its gaiety and its dread.

Notes and References

Preface

1. Julian Duplain, review, *Times Literary Supplement,* 5 March 1993.
2. Alan Brien, review, *Sunday Telegraph,* 10 August 1964, n.p.; hereafter cited in text.
3. Maurice Charney, *Joe Orton* (New York: Grove Press, 1984), 107; hereafter cited in text.

Chapter One

1. John Lahr, *Prick Up Your Ears* (New York: Alfred A. Knopf, 1978; second Limelight edition, 1991), 139; hereafter cited in text.
2. *The Orton Diaries,* ed. John Lahr (London: Methuen, 1986; Minerva reprint, 1989), 42; hereafter cited in text as *Diaries.*
3. Giles Gordon, interview, *Transatlantic Review* 24 (Spring 1967): 98; hereafter cited in text.
4. Ronald Bryden, review, *Observer,* 2 October 1966, n.p.
5. Terence Rattigan, *The Collected Works,* vol. 3 (London: Hamish Hamilton, 1964), xxxvii.
6. John Lahr, *Dame Edna Everage and the Rise of Western Civilization: Backstage with Barrie Humphries* (New York: Farrar, Straus & Giroux, 1992), 4; hereafter cited in text.

Chapter Two

1. W. A. Darlington, review, *Daily Telegraph,* 7 May 1964, n.p.; hereafter cited in text.
2. *Until She Screams* (sketch for the Kenneth Tynan revue *Oh, Calcutta!*), *Evergreen Review* 78 (May 1970): 51; hereafter cited in text as *Screams.*
3. Harold Pinter, *A Night Out, Night School, Revue Sketches, Early Plays* (New York: Grove Press, 1961), 98; hereafter cited in text.
4. *Head to Toe* (London: Methuen, 1986; New York: St. Martin's Press, 1986), 174; hereafter cited in text as *Head.*

Chapter Three

1. *Joe Orton: The Complete Plays* (London: Eyre Methuen, 1976; reprint, 1991), 143; hereafter cited in text as *Plays.*

2. *Up Against It: A Screenplay for the Beatles* (New York: Grove Press, 1979), 21; hereafter cited in text as *Against*.

3. Mel Gussow, review, *New York Times,* 5 December 1989, 17; hereafter cited in text.

Chapter Four

1. T. S. Eliot, "The Metaphysical Poets," in *Selected Essays of T. S. Eliot* (New York: Harcourt Brace, 1950), 243.

2. Irving Wardle, review of *Crimes of Passion,* London *Times,* 7 June 1967, 8; hereafter cited in text.

Chapter Six

1. John Russell Taylor, "Joe Orton," in *The Second Wave: New British Drama for the Seventies* (New York: Hill & Wang, 1971), 125; hereafter cited in text.

2. Quoted in James Fox, "The Life and Death of Joe Orton," *Sunday Times Magazine,* 22 November 1970, n.p.

3. Charles Marowitz, *Guardian,* 19 September 1966, n.p.

4. John Lahr, "Laughing It Off," *New Yorker,* 21 February 1994, 106; hereafter cited in text.

5. Walter Kerr, *Herald-Tribune,* 13 October 1965, n.p.

6. Howard Taubman, *New York Times,* 13 October 1965, n.p.

7. John Tillinger, *New York Times,* 7 April 1986, C23.

Chapter Seven

1. *Literary History of England,* ed. Albert C. Baugh (New York: Appleton-Century-Crofts, 1948), 566.

2. Irving Wardle, review, London *Times,* 4 June 1975, 12.

3. Mel Gussow, *New York Times,* 23 February 1986, H3.

4. Frank Rich, *New York Times,* 19 February 1986, C15.

5. Katharine J. Worth, "Form and Style in the Plays of Joe Orton," in *Modern British Dramatists,* ed. John Russell Brown (Englewood Cliffs, N.J.: Prentice-Hall, 1984), 76; hereafter cited in text.

6. *New York Times,* 17 November 1993, B5.

7. C. W. E. Bigsby, *Joe Orton* (London: Methuen, 1982), 41; hereafter cited in text.

8. John Simon, *New York Magazine,* 3 March 1986, 135; hereafter cited in text.

9. Oscar Wilde, *The Importance of Being Earnest,* in *Masterpieces of Modern Drama,* ed. John Gassner and Bernard Dukore (New York: Simon & Schuster, 1970), 253.

10.   Anthony Masters, review, London *Times,* 20 September 1984, 9.

Chapter Eight

1.   Hilary Spurling, "Young Master," *Spectator,* 14 March 1969, 344; hereafter cited in text.
2.   Frank Marcus, *Sunday Telegraph,* 9 March 1969, n.p.
3.   William Hutchings, "Joe Orton's Jacobean Assimilations in *What the Butler Saw,*" in *Themes of Drama,* vol. 10, *Farce,* ed. J. Redmond (Cambridge: Cambridge University Press, 1988), 228; hereafter cited in text.
4.   Leslie Smith, "Joe Orton," in *Modern British Farce* (Totowa, N.J.: Barnes & Noble, 1989), 131; hereafter cited in text.
5.   Irving Wardle, *Independent,* 5 March 1995, n.p.
6.   Benedict Nightingale, *Times,* 4 March 1995, 5.
7.   Michael Billington, *Guardian,* 4 March 1995, 28.

Chapter Nine

1.   Christopher Innes, "Joe Orton: Farce as Confrontation," in *Modern British Drama, 1890–1990* (Cambridge: Cambridge University Press, 1992), 277.
2.   Simon Trussler, interview in *Plays and Players,* June 1966, 72.

Selected Bibliography

PRIMARY WORKS

Joe Orton: The Complete Plays. London: Eyre Methuen, 1976; reprinted 1991.
Crimes of Passion: The Ruffian on the Stair and The Erpingham Camp. London: Methuen, 1967.
Entertaining Mr. Sloane. London: Hamish Hamilton, 1964; New York: Grove Press, 1964; London: Eyre Methuen, 1973.
Funeral Games and The Good and Faithful Servant. London: Methuen, 1970.
Head to Toe. London: Anthony Blond, 1971; London: Methuen, 1986; New York: St. Martin's Press, 1986.
Loot. London: Methuen, 1967; reprinted 1968.
The Orton Diaries. Edited by John Lahr. London: Methuen, 1986; Minerva, 1989; Methuen-Mandarin, 1989.
Until She Screams. A sketch for the Kenneth Tynan revue *Oh, Calcutta! Evergreen Review* 78 (May 1970): 51–53.
Up Against It: A Screenplay for the Beatles. London: Methuen, 1979.
What the Butler Saw. London: Methuen, 1969.

SECONDARY WORKS

Books

Bigsby, C. W. E. *Joe Orton.* Contemporary Writers Series. London: Methuen, 1982.
Charney, Maurice. *Joe Orton.* Modern Dramatists Series. New York: Grove Press, 1984.
Lahr, John. *Diary of a Somebody.* New York: Harper & Row, 1989; London: Methuen, 1989.
———. *Prick Up Your Ears.* London: Allen Lane, 1978; Harmondsworth: Penguin, 1978; New York: Alfred A. Knopf, 1978.

Articles and Parts of Books

Allen, M. D. "Joe Orton." In *Dictionary of Literary Biography,* edited by Stanley Weintraub, 13: 362–70. Detroit: Gale Research, 1982.
Barnes, Phillip. *A Companion to Post-War British Theatre,* 172–74. London: Croom Helm, 1986.

Bryden, Ronald. "On the Orton Offensive." *Observer,* 2 October 1966.

Casmus, Mary I. "Farce and Verbal Wit in the Plays of Joe Orton." *Journal of Popular Culture* 13 (1980): 461–68.

Draudt, Manfred. "Comic, Tragic, or Absurd? On Some Parallels between the Farces of Joe Orton and Seventeenth-Century Tragedy." *English Studies* 59 (1978): 202–17.

Esslin, Martin. "The Comedy of (Ill) Manners." In *Contemporary English Drama,* edited by C. W. E. Bigsby. London: Arnold, 1981; New York: Holmes & Meier, 1981.

Fraser, Kenneth. "Joe Orton: His Brief Career." *Modern Drama* 14 (1971): 413–19.

Gordon, Giles. "Joe Orton Interviewed by Giles Gordon." *Transatlantic Review* 24 (Spring 1967): 94–100.

Hutchings, Williams. "Joe Orton's Jacobean Assimilations in *What the Butler Saw.*" In *Themes in Modern Drama.* Vol. 10, *Farce,* edited by J. Redmond, 228–35. Cambridge: Cambridge University Press, 1988. Reprinted in *Drama Criticism,* 3: 419–25. Detroit: Gale Research, 1993.

Innes, Christopher. "Joe Orton: Farce as Confrontation." In *Modern British Drama, 1890–1990,* 268–78. Cambridge: Cambridge University Press, 1992.

Johnson, Patricia. "Money and Mr. Orton." *Evening News,* 9 June 1967.

Kerensky, Oleg. "Joe Orton." In *The New British Drama: Fourteen Playwrights since Osborne and Pinter.* London: Hamish Hamilton, 1977.

King, Kimball. *Twenty Modern British Playwrights: A Bibliography, 1956–1976,* 77–83. New York and London: Garland Publishing, 1977.

Lahr, John. Introduction. In *The Orton Diaries.* London: Methuen, 1986.

———. Introduction. In *Joe Orton: The Complete Plays.* London: Eyre Methuen, 1980.

———. Introduction. In *Up Against It: A Screenplay for the Beatles.* London: Eyre Methuen, 1979.

Marcus, Frank. "Comedy or Farce?" *London Magazine,* 6 February 1967, 73–77.

Marowitz, Charles. *"Entertaining Mr. Sloane." Guardian,* 19 September 1966.

Rusinko, Susan. "Joe Orton." In *British Drama, 1950 to the Present: A Critical History,* 87–95. Boston: Twayne Publishers, 1989.

Shepherd, Simon. "Edna's Last Stand: Joe Orton's Dialectic of Entertainment." *Renaissance and Modern Studies* 22 (1978): 87–130.

Smith, Leslie. "Democratic Lunacy: The Comedies of Joe Orton." *Adam International Review* 394–96 (1976): 73–92.

———. "Joe Orton." In *Modern British Farce,* 120–38. Totowa, N.J.: Barnes & Noble, 1989.

Spurling, Hilary. "Early Death." *Spectator,* 18 August 1967, 193.

———. "Young Master." *Spectator,* 14 March 1969, 344.

———. "The Late Lamented Joe Orton." *Plays and Players,* October 1970.

Taylor, John Russell. "Joe Orton." In *The Second Wave: New British Drama for the Seventies*, 125–40. New York: Hill & Wang, 1971.

———. Introduction. In *New English Dramatists*. Harmondsworth: Penguin, n.d.

Trussler, Simon. "The Biter Bit." *Plays and Players*, August 1964, 16.

———. Interview with Joe Orton. *Plays and Players*, June 1966, 56–58, 72.

———. "Joe Orton." In *Contemporary Dramatists*, 4th ed., edited by James Vinson. Chicago: St. James Press, 1988.

Worth, Katharine J. "Form and Style in the Plays of Joe Orton." In *Modern British Dramatists*, edited by John Russell Brown, 75–84. Englewood Cliffs, N.J.: Prentice-Hall, 1984.

Index

The Author

Susan Rusinko is emeritus professor and chair of the English Department at Bloomsburg University of Pennsylvania, where she taught modern drama and Russian literature and conducted biennial theater study trips to London. She received her B.A. from Wheaton College and her M.A. and Ph.D. from the Pennsylvania State University and is the author of critical studies on Terence Rattigan, Tom Stoppard, British drama since 1950, and Benn Levy. At Bloomsburg she continues her interest in the theater in an advisory capacity on university-sponsored trips to Stratford, Ontario, and Niagara-on-the-Lake.